I0187390

Student Leadership and Engagement in Post-Secondary Education

Submitted by Sam (Ajit) Thiara to the University of Exeter as a dissertation towards the degree of Master of Arts by advanced study in Leadership Studies, October, 2008

I certify that all material in this dissertation which is not my own work has been identified and that no material in included for which a degree has previously been conferred on me.

Copyright (c) 2016 by Sam Thiara

All rights reserved. No part of this publication may be reproduced or transmitted in any form or by any means, electronic or mechanical, including photocopying, recording, or by any information storage and retrieval systems, now known or to be invented, without permission in writing from the publisher.

First published in 2008

Ignite the Dream Consulting

Email: story.share.community@gmail.com

Web: http://sam-thiara.com

Twitter: @Sam_Thiara

10 9 8 7 6 5 4 3 2

ISBN - 978-0-9937581-2-6

Printed and bound in Canada by Lulu.com

Acknowledgements

I would like to acknowledge the following people who have supported me on this paper.

Gordon Barrett - who was my coach and friend through this process in Canada. He is someone who always made himself available to talk and work through the paper and gave up his own valuable time so that I might succeed.

My parents, for being the guides of my personal leadership development. They have instilled character, integrity, and values that have become the cornerstone of my life and that I can share with others to empower them to change in a positive way.

Finally the Students who participated in the research and those at SFU and across Canada who are the inspiration for this study. They are the ones who allow me to sit amidst them and see greatness every day and are the positive change that I dream about.

Dedication

This research project and the premise that is behind the study are dedicated to my wife Sadhna and our unborn child (Little T) who is due very soon. It has been a challenge to combine the work, this study, and concentrating on the birth of my first child, but as I have always said, it is through challenges that our greatest opportunities emerge.

It is hoped that this study will provide an environment of responsible leadership development so that "Little T" might grow up in a world where the emerging students from university are responsible leaders to guide society in a positive manner.

Table of Contents

Acknowledgements and Dedications 3

Abstract 7

Chapter 1- Introduction 8

    Research Aims 9

    Central Questions.. 9

    Motivation for Research.. 10

    The Importance of the Study and Its Contribution to Literature........................ 12

Chapter 2 – Literature Review 13

Introduction... 13

Background to the Research 13

    W.K. Kellogg Foundation Study... 14

The History of Student Leadership Development to the Present Day 15

    History of Student Leadership 16

    Boyer's Philosophy 21

    Examination of Student Leadership Theory 22

    Five Practices of Exemplary Student Leadership 23

    Relational Leadership.. 26

Examining University and Leadership Development 27

    Kotter's Change Model.. 27

    Collaboration... 29

    SFU Student Background... 32

Reflection on Literature Review 33

Summary 34

Chapter 3 – Methodology 35

Research Methodology.. 35

Focus Group Process... 35

    Structure of the Focus Groups 35

    Selection of the Students... 38

    Formulation of Research Questions... 39

    Facilitator Guidelines 40

Analysis of Results.. 42

Limitations and Biases of the Study 43

Personal Reflections on Methodology 44

Summary 45

Chapter 4 – Presentation of Results 47

Process Initiated 47

Overview of Focus Groups 48

    Focus Group Details.. 48

    Focus Group Mechanics.. 49

    Issues and Concerns.. 50

Outcome of Results Based on Questions Posed... 51

    Value of a Mission Statement 51

    Academic Studies and Leadership Development... 52

    Situational Leadership... 53

Leadership as a Process...55
Barriers to Student Leadership Development 56
  Time and Funding 57
  Cultural...57
Administration and Faculty..59
  Faculty Engagement...60
Observations...60
Summary 63
Chapter 5 – Discussion of Results..64
Collaboration..64
Relational Leadership...65
Influences 67
  Student and University...67
  Student Commitments Outside the Classroom 67
Student Leadership Influences 68
  Situational Leadership..69
  Self-serving Transformation to Engagement 70
  Servant Leadership...71
Influences on Students Not Getting Involved 71
  Time and Funding 72
  Cultural Implications..73
  Commuter Campus 73
The University Environment...74
  Flexibility versus Structure 75
  University Faculty Engagement...76
Academic Studies and Practical Experience 78
What I Have Learned and Contribution to Knowledge 80
Summary 81
Chapter 6 – Conclusion 82
Motivation for Research...83
Influences on Change 83
  Collaboration and Relationships 83
  Overcoming a Disconnect..84
  Self-serving Transformation 85
  Leadership Development and Academic Education 85
  Mission and Vision 86
  Diversification..86
The Importance of This Study..87
List of References 88
Appendices...92
Appendix A 93
  List of Tables..93
    Table 1 - Authors for the W.K Kellogg Paper 93
    Table 2 - Traditional Models of Leadership 93
    Table 3 - Contemporary Models of Leadership 94
    Table 4 - Hersey and Blanshard Model 94

Table 5 Academic and Practical Intelligence 95
Table 6 Kotter's Eight-Stage Process of Creating Major Change 95
Table 7 Applications to Integrate Student Leadership 96
Table 8 – SFU Student Profile from 2007 SFU Undergraduate Survey 96
Table 9 Gender demographics for focus group sessions 97
Table 10 – Breakdown of Focus Group Participants 97
Table 11 - Fall 2007 Undergraduate Student Survey on students working 98
Appendix B 99
   List of Figures 99
      Figure 1 Five Key Areas of Relational Leadership 99
      Figure 2. Venn diagram to illustrate when students are focused on their studies near
final exams 99
      Figure 3. Venn diagram to illustrate Student Focus Between Semesters 100
Appendix C 101
   Student Leadership and Engagement – Pre-screening Form 101
Appendix D 102
   Consent Form 102
Appendix E 103
Questions for Focus Groups 103
   Focus Group One and Two Guide Questions: 103
   Independent Response Supplementary Questions 103
   Focus Group Three Guide Questions: 104
Appendix F 105
   Results from Brainstorm Survey – Reasons for students enrolling at SFU 105

Abstract

This study examines students in a university setting in Canada and looks at their leadership and community involvement. It is the purpose of this study to examine what influences university students to get involved or not, so that universities can leverage the findings to influence a greater number of students in their leadership development.

This study incorporated three focus groups and a facilitator who led the groups through in-depth discussion of their understanding of leadership and community involvement. Some key concepts that emerged focused on a collaborative environment, relational leadership, an understanding of what influences students and the capacity of the university to create an environment of engagement.

Chapter 1- Introduction

You must be the change you wish to see.

(Gandhi, 1906)

There are three positions in society that one can take: to be a leader who is a catalyst for change, a follower who is part of change, or someone who watches change develop and lets it happen. This maxim also applies to learning about leadership. Post-secondary institutions have the ability to inspire, motivate, and educate students to enable them to become change agents. A university's responsibility is to provide a balanced environment that allows transformation to occur through academic education and engagement of individuals, who must apply the knowledge and experience gained to further their personal development.

From personal reflection on working in student development and observing numerous universities for many years, I can say that, historically, the balance of student development in Canadian and American universities has been skewed to focus primarily on theory, knowledge, and analysis in the student's area of study. Universities have not been proactive in the development of applied knowledge to develop young leaders. However, recently, North American post-secondary institutions are beginning to see the importance of developing their students' leadership skills in addition to academic success. (McDonald, 2002, pg 28) The Kellogg Foundation proposed that in order to garner positive change in the community, post-secondary institutions need to focus their attention on building programs that foster leadership development:

This is both an individual and an institutional challenge. Students will find it difficult to lead until they have experienced effective leadership as part of their education. They are not likely to commit to making changes in society unless the institutions in which they have been trained display a similar commitment.

(Kellogg Foundation, 2002, pg 2)

This implies an opportunity that can extend educational and leadership practice into the business world. Given the trend towards leadership development in Canadian universities, it is important to explore what influences students' perception of leadership, how it relates to their engagement, and how this might lead to universities being able to provide leadership opportunities to the larger population. Dunkle and Schuh suggest that students who are involved in campus organizations benefit substantially in their overall university experience. (Dunkle and Schuh, 1998, pg 3)

Research Aims

The focus of this study will be to understand what influences Canadian undergraduate university students to perceive themselves as leaders, or non-leaders, and how they apply leadership on campus and in the community. This research will provide a better understanding of how students develop leadership as part of their identity and provide insight into how universities can better leverage leadership opportunities for students.

Central Questions

In order to understand the influences upon students and their perception of leadership, the following questions will be addressed in the study:

- Can students identify and describe the significant influences on how they perceive and enact leadership in a community role context?

The following sub-questions will be addressed in this study to provide deeper analysis of the central question:

- What do students perceive as leadership?
- What community roles do the students take on and how do they describe them?
- How do students describe leadership and how it is enacted (including through their own and others' involvement) in these community contexts?
- What do students perceive as having been the major influences on them in undertaking leadership roles?
- What lessons can be drawn for the university to promote the active involvement of students in leadership roles?

This study will generate outcomes that will identify answers to:

- What attracted students to a leadership role?
- What influences students to undertake a leadership role?
- How might a university enable students to become more engaged in leadership activities and participate in leadership development programs?

Motivation for Research

The motivation for this research stems from the need of the university to examine both the effectiveness of its leadership programs and the impact that these programs have on student development. What needs to be examined is the combination of academic education and practical application in terms of leadership and engagement. There is a requirement for better bridging between academic education and practical 'real life' application, instead of having them run parallel to each other. This is best noted in the Student Affairs Officer position at Simon Fraser University, where I can experience student engagement first hand. The fundamental aim of this position is to work with students on their personal and professional development, and to complement their academic education by instituting programs that engage students in projects and initiatives, which develop their leadership potential. This is a situation in which the Student Affairs Officer creates and enacts leadership initiatives but there can be a limited understanding of the mechanics of engagement and student leadership.

When considering influences, it is important to see if there are any that emerge which are unique to a particular group, and that might be significantly different from a control group. As a result, focus groups will be the methodology of choice for this study and a group of second-generation Indo-Canadian university students will be one of the focus groups to see if the results they generate on leadership and influences are different from those of the control group of students who are a general representation of the population. The reason for the selection of a second-generation Indo-Canadian group is in part due to my background and understanding of the cultural implications of this group.

The consideration here is why I chose this topic and what it means to me personally. Where did this need come from? When I graduated from SFU in 1986, I had no level of support and felt that, after I graduated with my degree and alumni pin, the doors of the institution shut behind me and that I was now on my own. I put the alumni pin away in a safe place and I went away thinking to myself that, somewhere in the future, I would want to come back to this institution and work to make a difference so that students would not go through what I went through. Every so often, I would see the alumni pin and remember the promise I made to myself to come back to the university. Over the next 20 years in industry, I was resolved that the things I was doing, the experiences I encountered and the journey I was on had the ultimate aim of returning with all this knowledge to share. Assuming the Student Affairs position at Simon Fraser University, about 4 1/2 years ago, I went in wearing my SFU Alumni pin with the belief that I was empowered to make a difference. I did not go in thinking merely, "OK, let's see what the environment holds and see what I can do or if I will change lives." I went in with a specific mission to positively influence students and to get them engaged. (Thiara, Learning Log, July 27, 2008)

The Importance of the Study and Its Contribution to Literature

A university provides the opportunity to expand knowledge among youth by way of theory and academic education. In addition to traditional learning, there is a growing body of knowledge concerning leadership and its impact on student development such as Kouzes and Posner regarding The Student Leadership Challenge and William McDonald's Vision of Creating a Campus Community. By undertaking this study and examining the influences on student leadership, a contribution will be made and programs will be developed for students who are presently not engaged in leadership activities.

Chapter 2 – Literature Review

Introduction

There is a call for leaders to take charge at a time when there is a vacuum of leadership in our communities. Integrity, values, and norms appear to be at a low point when one reads or watches the news. One area that might provide an avenue for leadership development in a time of need is higher education. My experience in Student Affairs provides a glimpse of an area where leadership should be developed because there are individuals, like faculty and administrators, who embody a spirit and enthusiasm that can transform students to be the change. This leads to an opportunity to enhance students' personal and professional development for the benefit of the community at large.

There are countless studies and books on leadership that are trying to introduce numerous new concepts and ideas to an environment that seems ripe for leadership development. They speak about blending academic learning with practical application of leadership in the real world.

Background to the Research

An initial literature review revealed two key words that are woven into this study and which focus on what influences students to be involved and engaged. They appeared further in detailed literature reviews and then reappeared in the methodology. The two words are 'collaboration' and 'relationships'. My foundation of student leadership development, paired with the literature review, indicates that collaboration and establishing solid relationships work in unison. Other concepts and thoughts emerged, but they all seem to connect in one way or another to building a collaborative environment through relationships.

W.K. Kellogg Foundation Study

These fundamental thoughts about collaboration and relationships emerged from a comprehensive resource on university leadership development and transformative impacts on student engagement. Much of the foundation of this research emerged from the W.K Kellogg Foundation study called 'Leadership Reconsidered: Engaging Higher Education in Social Change', which proved to support key aspects of my own study. The Kellogg study will be referenced throughout this research project. What is interesting about this resource is that it provides a qualitative and quantitative assessment of student leadership development. The document by the Kellogg Foundation draws on a number of contributing authors who are recognized for their experience in leadership development (see Appendix A Table 1). Another aspect of the Kellogg Foundation study is that it looked at a shared responsibility for leadership development rather than a responsibility that rests on one part of the institution. It addresses the need for collaboration on the part of all parties concerned and, as will be discussed, a collaborative environment is what many experts are suggesting needs to be pursued. This 2000 Kellogg Foundation document consists of the following chapters:

- The need for change,
- The view of transformative leadership,
- Students' capacity to change the institution,
- The leadership role of the faculty,
- A look at student affairs professionals in the field of leadership development,
- The president of the institution and their responsibility
- A collective view how all can come together to transform the institution.

It takes the approach that the university is a bigger institution than any one player and that all parties have a responsibility to provide students with the best available tools for leadership development, leading to the transformation of the student.

A limitation of this resource is that it was conducted in United States, so some of the findings may have limited applications to other societies. Another limitation is that the study is becoming dated as it was conducted almost nine years ago. In spite of these limitations, the Kellogg Foundation provides great insight and reveals a solid foundation for universities to consider when revising their leadership development. A further advantage of the study is that it incorporates the work of some of the key researchers in student leadership development, such as Alexander and Helen Austin, John Burkhardt, and Kathleen Zimmerman-Oster to name a few, who are represented by other references used in this study.

The History of Student Leadership Development to the Present Day

In order to apply the concepts of collaboration and relational leadership to student leadership development, there is a need to understand the history of university student engagement and explore how these concepts can penetrate and integrate with the university environment and benefit the community.

Leadership research has developed over time from a point of limited understanding to a much wider base of research. One area of leadership study that is still in its infancy is the development of student leaders in post secondary education. Universities and colleges have created formal curricular and co-curricular programs; however, there has been limited development of the student, institution and the community outcomes.

> Research universities have been somewhat slower than liberal arts colleges in helping faculty integrate concepts of ethical behaviour, personal integrity, character development, and an appreciation of diversity as components of leadership into a curricular perspective.
>
> (McDonald, 2002, pg 28)

Regarding this statement, there is a growing understanding within the research community, student development departments and business schools that universities need to take a more active role and responsibility in community engagement and student leadership development. This is evident from the creation of the Student Affairs position at Simon Fraser University (SFU). This is also apparent from the increase in the amount of research conducted on student leadership development and the increasing interest that universities, such as SFU, have taken in reviewing their student leadership development programs. There is a need to shift to a position more in line with the following:

> Viewed in this context, an important "leadership development" challenge for higher education is to empower students, by helping them develop those special talents and attitudes that will enable them to become effective social change agents.
>
> (Kellogg Foundation, 2002, pg 2)

This expresses the fundamental aspect of empowering students to be the change in their communities and universities.

History of Student Leadership

In the past, a definition of leadership would describe leadership as one person being at the helm and commanding followers' attention to execute a project.

> Early definitions...typically describe leadership as one person controlling others or inducing them to follow his or her command.
>
> (Komives, Lucas and McMahon, 1998, pg 31)

Most theories in the past looked at leadership as a one-dimensional phenomenon, of the leader having sole control over providing change. Traditional models of leadership, from Phase 2 – Week 2 of the University of Exeter Centre for Leadership Studies, included traditional aspects such as traits, skills and the behavioural and situational (contingency) approaches. (See Appendix A Table 2). Views mentioned in these examples put the leader in the sole position of power and demonstrate either the self or the situation, but are focused on one person and not the individuals around the leader.

Contemporary models of leadership shift to a participative approach which are more inclusive and, in them, the leader and followers work together to accomplish a goal, reinforcing the aspect of developing a collaborative environment. The emphasis is more on the follower being participative, and part of the desired change.

> Another common aspect of most current definitions is that there is a level of interaction between leaders and followers who are working together to accomplish a goal or some type of action, and the interaction often is based on some type of influence.
>
> (Komives, Lucas, McMahon, 1998, pg 31)

This concept is reinforced when considering contemporary models of leadership provided by the University of Exeter Centre for Leadership Studies, models such as the charismatic, the transformational, the leader as follower and distributed leadership. (See Appendix A Table 3). This demonstrates that there has been a shift from sole power to shared power, except in the case of Charismatic Leadership. The concept of a leader embodying charisma includes the motivation of others by one person at the top, but in this case, his or her principle aim is to motivate others, so there is an involvement of followers in the desired outcome.

Moving from transformational to distributed leadership, one can see relational and collaborative aspects starting to surface. A model that shows this progression would be the Hersey and Blanchard Leadership Model (1996, 1977, 1988) in which they talk about directive and supportive behaviour. (See Appendix A Table 4).

Taking the Hersey and Blanchard model further, an example of this progression from directive to supportive behaviour can be seen in a study by the 2006 National Survey of Student Engagement, which applied to the University of Windsor. They compared first year students to final year students in areas outside the classroom. The most prevalent issue for first year students was the provision of increased contact with professors outside the classroom. For final year students, it was about providing students with more opportunities to undertake research with faculty (University of Windsor, 2006, pg 14). This outlined a need on the part of the students to move from a more directive, one- way communication track, to a more participative and involved role.

The one caution here is that, while leadership is becoming more participatory and collaborative, as described in Komives, Lucas and McMahon, the pursuit of noble goals may not always be the case.

> … leadership is best described as using your personal philosophy of how to work effectively with others towards meaningful change.
>
> (Komives, Lucas and McMahon, 1998, pg 11)

There are organizations in a university that demonstrate participatory leadership; however, they are more focused on their own personal development or organizational needs.

> However, by and large, the tie that binds men and women in organizations today, particularly at the professional and managerial levels, is narrow self-interest, rather than a sense of mutual obligations and responsibilities.
>
> (Zaleznik, 1990, pg 7)

This indicates that, while the goal of engagement can arise from a desire to benefit the community, there are instances where the underlying motivation to be engaged can be because of self-interest. What is interesting about this is that engagement may involve collaboration and relationships within the group, but this may not extend externally when considering related stakeholders. One such example at a university might be a student club on campus that puts its mandate ahead of a common purpose. This might be due to limited financial resources or the mandate of the elected president. It brings to light the fact that there are often unavoidably competing, but balancing, circumstances.

> In a healthy democracy, for example, there is a need to balance those competing ideas and impulses that are philosophic anchors for a democracy – the balance between access and excellence in education, rights and responsibility, justice and mercy, diversity and community, opportunity and disciplined effort, cooperation and competition, service and profit, self-interest and self-sacrifice, tradition and innovation.
>
> (McDonald, 2002, pg 3)

We cannot strive for a society that tilts in just one direction. Re-examining Hersey and Blanchard's model on leader behaviours, it is understandable that there will always be organizations that are both directive and at the same time participative. There is, for example, the flexibility of the Student Affairs position at SFU, in contrast to the directive academic experience of a faculty member teaching a finance course. In this situation, there is a need for universities to provide experiential learning that is more focused on participative opportunities but which still blends with the academic studies so that they complement each other.

It would appear that, while studies on student leadership are being examined, this does not mean that the results are applied in a practical sense. A study by the Kellogg Foundation determined that co-curricular experiences for students in post-secondary education create an environment rich in the development of leadership that can be sustained and yet many post secondary institutions do not offer an environment for student leadership development. (Kellogg Foundation, 2000, pg 3)   One study that puts things into perspective, in the enhancement and development frame for student involvement, is the Sanford study of 1966 in which three conditions for engagement are outlined:

1) Readiness – (the person). Where individuals cannot change until they are ready to do so.
2) Environmental challenges (external) – For a change to occur, there must be internal or external stimuli, which upset [the student's] equilibrium.
3) Support - (balance) To achieve an optimal level of dissonance, challenge in the environment must be balanced by support.

(Hamrick, Evans and Schuh, 2002, pg 82)

This study introduces and expands on the collaborative environment that is required today to provide a rich environment fostering leadership development. It involves the person, the environment and the institution. As will be discussed later, a collaborative environment is critical, as stated in the Kellogg Foundation study:

Probably all of the modern authorities on leadership, regardless of whether they focus on the corporate world or the non-profit sector, now advocate a collaborative approach to leadership, as opposed to one based on power and authority.

(Kellogg Foundation, 2002, pg 4)

This is also reinforced by the Hersey and Blanchard model discussed earlier.

It is evident that, while universities are established to provide academic education and are environments of learning, when it comes to practical application and development of students as leaders, there are limitations in place. This is due in part to the difference between academic intelligence and practical intelligence. For the Robert Stenberg outline of the differences, see Appendix A Table 5.

Examining this concept, it is apparent that practical intelligence embodies academic intelligence and is an important concept to consider since universities are often focused more on academic intelligence and less involved in practical intelligence. Based on this, it is apparent that academic intelligence is more about the self while practical intelligence is about the relations we build, based on our application of the academic and practical experiences.

Boyer's Philosophy

As discussed earlier, collaboration is complemented by relationships and relational leadership and this section expands on how these concepts are required for an environment that is more conducive to student leadership development in a university. To better understand the nature of a university environment and how this might influence student leadership development, Ernest Boyer outlined various relational characteristics of a university or college as:

- A purposeful community – where students and faculty share learning goals and where community begins. This is classroom and learning based
- An open community – about freedom of expression
- A just community – prejudice and arrogance are not accepted
- A disciplined community – students accept their obligations and there are well defined regulations that must be followed
- A caring community – there is a connection between the student and the campus
- A celebrative community – the campus heritage and tradition are established and central to the institutions identity

(McDonald, 2002, pg 8)

These characteristics become a foundation for examination of a university and leadership development implications for students based on the relationships that are established. One limitation of this model is that it only encompasses the university community and not the external stakeholder relationships, which are equally important. Boyer's foundation starts within the classroom and expands through the administration and mission/values of the university but it stops there. SFU recently did a study in 2000 on its direct and indirect economic impact on the greater Vancouver area, to better understand the external impact the university might have. The direct impact, which refers to SFU's operations and employment concerned with the running of the university, on the community around it added up to $228 million. An assessment regarding the indirect impact was noted at $112 million. (Chan, March 2000, pg 9) This indicates the importance of the relationships established external to the institution. It can be argued that, with recent trends at SFU, there is an even greater impact on the community at large, considering programs like the Student Affairs Office, LEAD – leadership training, and a university-wide volunteer coordination office, to name a few.

Examination of Student Leadership Theory

The foundation of leadership in universities rests with administrators, faculty and staff, who have the task of running the university but need to constantly bear in mind that they are there to serve the needs of the students who are to become emerging leaders.

> Colleges and universities exist for purposes beyond developing knowledge and skill in our students. They are also sanctuaries of our personal and civic values, incubators of intellect and integrity.
>
> (McDonald, 2002, pg 8)

The university needs to create an environment of and provide opportunities for engagement. It has been proven that when university students are involved and engaged in projects, there is a direct correlation to leadership development.

There is a comprehensive study called "Student Experience and Satisfaction", and in that study, it was documented that student involvement contributed to the students' leadership development.

(McDonald, 2002, pg 36)

When considering student leadership development, social identity is an important concept that brings relational views and group dynamics together through personal and social identity. Personal identity comprises the individual characteristics intrinsic to students and social identity is about their self-perception as members in a social group. (McShane, 2004, pg 74) It is the combination of personal interactions combined with group dynamics, which becomes the foundation of various theories, and provides an idea of how student lives are multi-dimensional and impacted by their personal and social interactions. This provides an understanding of the students' own inputs and the group interactions that have an effect on the students' experiences in leadership development, and reinforces the importance of collaboration and relationships.

Five Practices of Exemplary Student Leadership

From a Student Affairs perspective, one can be immersed in student engagement but sometimes unsure of the mechanisms that lead to better understanding of student involvement. One source that provides a model that assists this understanding is the work of Kouzes and Posner, which indicates that there are Five Practices of Exemplary Student Leadership, which emerged from conducting thousands of surveys and interviews. These are:

- Model the way
- Inspire a shared vision
- Challenge the process
- Enable others to act

- Encourage the heart.

(Kouzes and Posner, 2006, pg 1-6)

What Kouzes and Posner examine is a personal view of what a student leader needs to bring forward to be successful and also that there is a relationship between those who lead and those who follow, built on establishing a foundation of creating a collaborative environment. What adds value to the Five Practices is that there is a qualitative and quantitative assessment that they have undertaken to come up with the practices. By providing the Five Practices, Kouzes and Posner allow a student to find a path towards leadership development with a proven model to follow.

The Five Practices of Exemplary Student Leadership establishes a personal solid foundation of leadership so that students can mobilize others to benefit the community. These become the foundations from which a person can lead and inspire others. Kouzes and Posner speak about inspiring a shared vision, and that it is in pursuit of the common good and for noble ends.

> Leaders forge a unity of purpose by showing constituents how the dream is
> for the common good.

(Kouzes and Posner, 2006, pg 3)

A challenge to this theory is observable in the university setting where people are undertaking leadership roles for self-serving reasons such as padding their resume or their own view of what should be done, as indicated in the discussion of participative leadership.

The positive side of Kouzes and Posner's Five Practices demonstrates these principles are not reserved for the few to lead the masses, it provides the tools and guidelines so that leadership is attainable for anyone who would like to get involved. The five aspects that Kouzes and Posner mention, allows students to build their confidence in taking on leadership roles, and to be ready to jump at responsibilities as they come forward based on experience demonstrating leadership such as servant leadership. Grizzell defined servant leadership as:

> Servant leadership pushes for a moral community that shapes character and behavior, a community that serves as a stabilizing force in society – a community that focuses on the worth and value of people, a community with a soul.

> (Grizzell, 2008, pg 1)

Some find servant leadership and modelling to be the way to express their leadership and this results in others taking on a challenge, because of the concept of giving back and seeing people give of themselves.

Another challenge for the Five Practices of Exemplary Student Leadership has reference to the fact that ethnic background is not necessarily a block to engaging in these five areas.

> Moreover, the ability to engage in The Five Practices of Exemplary Student Leadership is not related to following a particular course of study or major, GPA, gender, ethnic background, or personality variable.

> (Kouzes and Posner. 2006, pg 7)

It can be argued that students of non-Western ethnic background might find it difficult to initiate the Five Practices of Student Leadership because they find it difficult to adapt to Western views of university life and as such, might feel marginalized or not fully understand the reasons for getting involved in extra-curricular activities.

> Some researchers, however, have questioned the effectiveness of traditional leadership programs based on hierarchical conceptions of leadership that might marginalize students of color.

> (Ortiz, Ah-Nee Benham, Cress, Langdon and Yamasaki, 1999)

> (Lin, 2007, pg 3)

It is not as easy for these students to start university and step into the five considerations that Kouzes and Posner outline. As the Student Affairs Officer, I have personally experienced students' difficulties in integrating into the university system. This is because some students of some ethnic and cultural backgrounds need to first establish a basic sense of belonging in order to transition into a level of engagement:

> Many students from minority groups see themselves as an outsider throughout the college years, while other students (new freshmen, or transfers who are members of a dominant group) might feel temporarily marginalized.
>
> (Hamrick, Evans, Schuh, 2002, pg 86)

It is more than that just the need to find their niche. It is worth noting that a limitation of this study is that it does not treat the ethnic/cultural or social implications of student leadership and engagement in depth, but it is worth examining in brief, and this does emerge as an influence in this study.

Relational Leadership

A counterpoint to Kouzes and Posner's Five Practices of Exemplary Leadership was a concept that Komives, Lucas and McMahon brought forward on Relational Leadership. They define relational leadership as:

> A relational process of people together attempting to accomplish change or make a difference to benefit the common good.
>
> (Komives, Lucas and McMahon, 1998, pg 21)

It is felt that leadership has its foundation in relationships between people striving to the benefit of the common good. Komives, Lucas and McMahon felt that there is neither one way to lead nor a checklist that states whether a person is an accomplished leader. They emphasise more how everyone's talents, along with their ethical and inclusive contributions, should be brought to the forefront to create socially responsible change.

(Komives, Lucas and McMahon, 1998, pg 21) Leadership is not necessarily a formula that is impacted by the environment, situation, culture and other factors. As discussed earlier, many of the students who first become engaged and are influenced by a group are interested simply in the aspect of belonging, or in finding something that looks good on their resume. It is once they get firmly got involved and build up experience that this motivation is transformed into the idea that it is for the common good and becomes collaborative, based on the relationships established.

Examining University and Leadership Development

It is apparent from the research done that universities needed to turn their attention from researching student leadership development and move towards a more proactive approach of implementing programs and change that foster further leadership development of their students. As noted, collaboration and the development of relationships can become the foundation of the transformation of the student, getting them involved in the community. The Student Affairs position provides first hand experience of how a university has the capacity to create programs that engage students. What is required is to understand how a university might go about creating a process of change so that it fosters an environment that is rich in student involvement.

Kotter's Change Model

When looking at change and how a university might integrate a process of change, John Kotter's Eight-Stage process of creating major change should be considered as an example because it brings forward the strength of collaboration and relationships as the cornerstone of change and, for a university, this could create a transformative environment for the students around the issue of engagement. Kotter outlined eight steps to change. (See Appendix A Table 6)

The first four points start the change process, while stages five to seven introduce the new practices and, finally, stage eight ensures sustainability. (Kotter, 1996, pg 22)

Kotter advises that all of the steps must be followed in sequence in order for the change to be successful and lasting. A drop in effort along the way or skipping steps due to pressure from the environment will not result in the desired outcomes that will lead to positive change. (Kotter, 1996, pg 24) The reason Kotter's process is worth considering is that it provides a step-by-step approach that a university, or faculties within a university could consider. Examining the university environment, the possible limitation might be departmental self-interest and lack of communication, but if they can work together, the possibility for a substantial change is far reaching. The Kellogg Foundation outlines a specific aspect that seems to impact directly on what Kotter suggests,

> In particular, there are three types of traditions that can actually facilitate the practice of transformative leadership: new starts, celebrations and statements of institutional mission.
>
> (Kellogg Foundation, 2000, pg 90)

These are examples that can initiate the change process because they provide an opportunity for partnerships, which become the focus of creating a collaborative environment, to be established.

An example of an organization looking at change lies in the Inter-professional Education area. The recommendations of Hoffman et al suggest four practical actions that can be considered for reforming universities. (See Appendix A Table 7)

They recognized the need for change based on relationships and collaboration and that this leads to transformative leadership development of their students. Kotter would argue that there are further steps required for sustainability; however, this does indicate that there are post-secondary institutions that are on the path of change.

Collaboration

Being a part of the university as the Student Affairs Officer, I can identify two aspects of collaboration that apply to the leadership development of the student. One is the collaborative path, that the students work towards, which we have spoken about, and the other is a collaborative environment in the university. Establishing a collaborative university community allows the development of student engagement because it encourages individuals to bring forward their strengths in an environment that accepts and encourages transformative change.

One reason why collaboration has been difficult to institute in a university environment is that all too often, university departments are protective of their respective areas and do not advance the main reason they are in existence, which is to benefit the students. The Kellogg Foundation described universities as organized into administrations with a chain of command and arranged with a hierarchy where:

> Individualism also makes collaboration difficult because it tends to breed competitiveness.
>
> (Kellogg Foundation, 2000, pg 6)

If organizations are not working in collaboration, then it means that faculties, administration, and departments all work in silos and through self-interest. Collaboration, according to Kouzes and Posner may be defined as:

> Collaboration is the critical competency for achieving and sustaining high performance – especially in the Internet Age! It won't be the ability to fiercely compete but the ability to lovingly cooperate that will determine success.
>
> (Kouzes and Posner, 2002, pg 242)

What is interesting about the idea of collaboration in a university setting is that it creates the foundations for implementing the changes that Kotter spoke about in his 'Eight Stage Process to Create Major Change'. Collaboration creates an environment that pulls the institution together to initiate change so that there is open communication both internally and externally.

Related to the concept of collaboration were the ideas of relational leadership that Komives, Lucas and McMahon put forward earlier.

> We view leadership as a relational process of people together attempting to accomplish change or make a difference to benefit the common good.
> (Komives, Lucas and McMahon, 1998, pg 68)

They suggest that this model is not a leadership theory but rather a framework, which connects five elements to a process. (Komives, Lucas and McMahon, 1998, pg 69) It continues the theme of collaboration because it seeks to understand leadership as being based on the relationships that we establish with this in turn fostering change when applied to Kotter's change model.

Relational Leadership involves five key areas of influence. (See Appendix B Figure 1)

- Inclusive
- Empower
- Purposeful
- Ethical
- Process oriented

Examining the five areas of influence, the inclusive aspect means respecting and understanding multiple perspectives. 'Empowerment' means providing authorization to all people involved to be able to take action. The term 'purposeful' is about a commitment to a goal or activity. Considering the ethical aspect, it is about values and standards in place. Finally, the term 'process-oriented' is about how the group goes about accomplishing a purpose. (Komives, Lucas and McMahon, 1998, pg 73-94) What I appreciate about this model is that it provides an inclusive perspective that builds on the relationships that we have spoken about. It sets the base from which collaboration can be built.

When considering a university environment, relational leadership is an important concept to take into account because, as stated by the W.K. Kellogg Report, there are a number of relationships that make up the entire university community. This includes the students, faculty, administration, student affairs, and external stakeholders. These units are all related to each other and the collective strength of these units creates an environment that can incorporate change towards student development. Rost's definition supports this:

> ...leadership is an influence relationship among leaders and followers who intend real changes that reflect their mutual purposes.
>
> (Brungardt, 1998, pg 2)

An understanding of Relational Leadership moves from the traditional approach of university administrations and individuals working in silos to one where partnerships are established. Student leadership programs are better able to develop and flourish when the environment allows the various stakeholders to work with each other for the benefit of the students.

A final overarching concept to examine, when looking at student leadership development based on collaboration and relational leadership, is the acknowledged mission statement of the institution. The mission statement outlines the position of the university and provides direction on the leadership development of students. Zimmerman-Oster and Burkhardt state:

> The development of leadership among college students is one of the goals often cited in the mission statements of higher education institutions.
>
> (Zimmerman-Oster and Burkhardt, 1999, pg 51)

It is clear that the mission statement is important for all stakeholders to understand and that it will reflect the university's position on student development; however, Simon Fraser University does not have its mission statement accessible on the SFU web page. This creates concerns; the university's mission statement is not readily available to indicate how students factor into the overall university community.

SFU Student Background

Before attempting to address the research question to the methodology, an understanding of the background of SFU is required. SFU is a recognized interdisciplinary post-secondary institution in Burnaby, B.C., created in the 1960's. Currently there are approximately 26,000 active students. The Canadian University Survey Consortium (CUSC) has conducted a thorough survey of university students in Canada. In June 2008, the survey stated the following:

> The typical undergraduate student is a 22-year-old female. Indeed, female students outnumber male students by two to one…for the most part, the experience, attitudes of female students appear to be similar to those of male students. Overall, 19% of students report being part of an ethnic or cultural group that might be considered visible minority...
>
> (Canadian University Consortium, June 2008, pg i)

This study was conducted Canada-wide and SFU participated in the survey. The survey was web based and there were 1,000 questionnaires distributed, of which 294 were completed for a 29.4% response rate. SFU is considered a Group 2 university, which is a university that provides undergraduate and graduate studies and is considered a medium sized university based on student population. (Canadian University Consortium, June 2008, pg 5) A more specific SFU Survey has been done, the Fall 2007 SFU Undergraduate Student Survey. A total of 3,355 students participated in the survey, which yielded a 15.4% response rate. (See Appendix A Table 8). (Institutional Research and Planning, Simon Fraser University, Fall 2007, pg 1)

Reflection on Literature Review

Very early in the literature review, there were two key themes that emerged that I realized were not so prevalent in the university environment. They are collaboration and relational leadership. Drawing on my experiences in student development as the Student Affairs Officer, I saw at first hand how a university functions, and how it can miss the mark on creating the structures that will benefit students in their quest for leadership. The journals and books were selected for this study because of the implications of their research on the aspect of student leadership development

Regarding the concepts of collaboration and relational leadership, there are two areas to concentrate on, one is student leadership development and the other is its application in universities. The sources selected provided background understanding of the current thoughts on student leadership development by applying them to the student and the university. Developing personal knowledge in this subject, for me as a researcher and the Student Affairs Officer, has allowed me to have a better grasp of the concepts and ideas that relate to this paper's research question. The literature review has allowed me to be informed so that I can examine the results within the framework of the body of knowledge on student leadership development, and speak to the results with some authority. This will allow the results of this paper to contribute to the wider body of knowledge. Finally, the sources also provide a foundation for knowledge in student leadership development, which will directly affect my day-to-day functioning as the Student Affairs Officer.

Summary

Two key terms emerged for consideration in this study; they are collaboration and relational leadership, which affect the university student in the area of student leadership development. The W.K. Kellogg study on student leadership provided significant insight. This was complemented by literature on relational leadership, Kotter's '8 Steps to Change' and Kouzes and Posner's 'Five Practices of Student Leadership'. Other supporting books, articles and information have been applied to the remainder of this study.

Chapter 3 – Methodology
Research Methodology

As the Student Affairs Officer, my mandate is to engage all students in leadership development; however, sometimes plans are established about what is deemed necessary for student involvement without consulting the target audience. To understand what might influence a student to get involved or not, it makes sense to research at the source and talk to students. To have an organized and meaningful dialogue, it is advantageous to employ the process of focus groups since this allows for discussion and reflection by the students on their personal leadership development, and the results can be applied to the research question. I have learned a lot by going through this process.

For the purpose of this study, focus group discussion provided both the opportunity to follow up questions that emerged during interaction and to observe the participants directly, which facilitated the application of inductive and interpretive research. Regarding student leadership as a construct, there was a need to provide a forum of discussion to examine what influences students to get involved and to explore their perceptions of what leadership means in a university setting.

Focus Group Process

For the benefit of this study, an approach was adopted that was based on considerations such as the structure of focus groups, selection of participants, formulation of research questions and facilitator guidelines.

Structure of the Focus Groups

At the outset, a request to participate in the study was forwarded to students via email, Facebook invitation and by word of mouth. This was done throughout the university and not concentrated in one area. The importance of this was to provide a sample size that was diverse, representing the student demographics. Students were provided with the dates of the various focus groups and were asked to contact the facilitator so that the facilitator could forward a pre-screening form. (See Appendix C)

The study incorporated the use of three focus groups. The first focus group was a control group made up of a diverse sample of students. The second focus group was made up of Indo-Canadian students and their discussion was based on the questions identical to those put to focus group One. Both focus group sessions were conducted on the same day.

The third focus group, which was to meet about two weeks later, was made up of new students who had not participated in any of the previous focus groups. The reason for this was that, if all focus groups were conducted with the same questions, there would not be an opportunity to ask deeper questions on influences, leadership and the university, arising from any notable results that emerged from discussion. Reserving a third focus group for further investigation based on a new set of questions provided the ability for detailed exploration based on the results of the first two focus groups.

To try to maintain the reliability of the data, rather than base all assessment solely on the use of focus groups, a secondary test was implemented where feedback on influences and leadership was requested from an independent group of students outside of any focus group. The reason for this method was that it allowed a way for the focus group results to be compared to another form of data. A secondary request through email and Facebook for students to provide their insight was provided. According to Stewart, Shamdasani and Rook, this was a good way to limit the groupthink bias:

> Fern (1982) tested this acquaintanceship assumption and concluded that an aggregation of the independent responses of individuals who are unknown to one another and who do not meet as a group is just as effective for generating ideas as focus groups.
>
> (Stewart, Shamdasani and Rook, pg 207)

The responses from these independent students are also referenced in the study, where applicable, confirming or refuting information provided by the three focus groups.

Trying to line up three focus groups was a challenge, considering the time of the year that the request went out, the timing of the actual focus groups, commitments that students already had, and so on; however, there was enough interest on the part of the students to provide meaningful insight.

This study required approval from the university ethics committee before it could be initiated since it involved human subjects. Anonymity of focus group participants was a priority to maintain their confidentiality, and all information was recorded but names were not provided in the writing up of the study. Primary approval came from the University of Exeter and, since the research involved undergraduate students from Simon Fraser University, secondary approval was required from this institution.

Each focus group session was scheduled for two hours, of which one and a half hours were dedicated to the actual discussion, with a buffer of half an hour if needed. It was important to keep in mind that while there was a set time limit in place, the priority was the quality of discussion initiated and not just trying to get the maximum amount of questions considered. Recording of the discussion was in audio only; this was less conspicuous than using video recording and provided a higher degree of anonymity over video recording. This also allowed focus group participants to concentrate more closely on the questions posed and not on the technical equipment and its operation.

At any time during the focus group, if a member felt that they did not want to participate, they had the option to excuse themselves and there were no consequences. Even though they had the option, no participant left any of the focus group sessions. A sample of the consent form that outlines this is provided in Appendix D.

Selection of the Students

At the outset, students interested in participating in the focus group sessions were forwarded a pre-screening form. The use of the pre-screening forms was required to determine which student would be placed in which focus group. The ideal of the focus group design was to represent the gender and age of the university demographics as provided in Chapter Two.

Students were asked to fill in a form with a coded number to protect their anonymity. The form captured biographical data such as age, gender and cultural background and so on. Students interested in participating in the focus group were provided a preliminary verbal introduction on what the study was about.

Focus group One involved a random selection of students in the undergraduate program at Simon Fraser University and this became the control group. The second group consisted of Indo-Canadian university students of second generation origin currently attending Simon Fraser University as undergraduate students. If there were limited responses in the participation of focus group Two, made up of this ethnic group, a back-up plan allowed for the expansion of the participants to include Asian students meeting the same criteria as the Indo-Canadian group. The second focus group members were to have the majority of their education in Canada and would not be of any particular ethnic group of Indo-Canadians. What this meant was that they might be Hindu, Muslim, Sikh or any other group associated with the region. The reason for the selection of a specific ethnic group was to determine if their influences differed from the first, control focus group.

Formulation of Research Questions

The research questions considered for this study focused on student leadership and what influenced students to get involved. An added component addressed the university and how it might leverage those influences to create programs that further engaged students. While the primary questions considered for all three focus groups were created for determining such influences, the actual discussion and interactions during each focus group allowed for deeper exploration through the asking of secondary questions.

A complete list of primary questions asked of focus groups One and Two are provided in the appendices (see Appendix E). The questions that were asked in focus groups One and Two had a progression in which the first series of open-ended questions established a base for the group on what their understanding of leadership was. The importance of starting at this point was that, through discussion, participants developed a general sense of leadership. This allowed the participants to formulate a basic shared understanding of what leadership meant to each person. It was also a straightforward line of questions that allowed all participants to bring their own insight to the discussion.

The next series of questions concentrated on influences, what students would determine as their level of involvement and why they would or would not be engaged in an activity outside the classroom. The emphasis was on starting to understand what prompted students to be engaged and where these tendencies might emerge. In order to personalize it further, the participants were asked to reflect on personal examples that they might want to share. The reason for this reflective exercise in questioning was to go beyond the standard theoretical explanations of leadership. It allowed the opportunity to explore practical definitions and understandings of leadership.

Focus group Three questions emerged out of the discussions that took place in focus groups One and Two. After analyzing what was discussed by both focus groups, a series of questions was developed by the facilitator that looked at further questions that might not have been fully answered by the previous groups. It also allowed the facilitator to see any patterns or variances and explore the results more deeply. The questions were arranged in a specific manner, which centred on the student first and then went into their experiences with the university. (See Appendix E)

In addition, a series of independent responses were also gathered to supplement the focus group questions. Three questions were provided to these independent individuals. (See Appendix E) These three questions provided enough exposure to the subject for students to provide their own insights, independent of anyone else, since these were received as email responses. Again, the progression of questions was designed to gain understanding of what the influences were, where they emerged from, and what the university needed to consider.

Facilitator Guidelines

Providing control of the focus group process and discussion, and applying the knowledge gained to the study. I was the facilitator. The importance of this was the experience I have built up through being the Student Affairs Officer for the last 4 ½ years.

Even before the focus groups started, the facilitator selected the students who participated in the focus group discussion by way of pre-screening forms. If there were any queries by focus group participants, the facilitator answered their questions.

The facilitator guided the discussion of the focus groups based on the questions posed to the students in all three sessions. Added to this, the role of the facilitator was to ensure that the discussion did not go off topic. The facilitator directed questions based on the needs of the groups and a key role of this person was to make sure that all participants had an opportunity to provide their input, ensuring that just a few participants did not dominate the discussion. Added to this, an environment needed to be established that allowed students to speak freely and not feel that others would judge them or put them into an uncomfortable situation.

During the focus groups, the facilitator maintained the time keeping so that the sessions would be no more than three hours in length. The facilitator allowed discussion to take place but at the same time, took the overall flow of discussion into account so that the questions could be asked in the allotted time.

To ensure limited bias and a better method of data collection, an assistant facilitator was included. This enabled me to concentrate on the focus group sessions and discussion and not to be involved with the recording of the results. While an audio recording device was used during the focus group sessions, the assistant facilitator was also responsible for scribing information. Furthermore, the assistant facilitator made certain that the gathering would be conducted within the time allotted and that the facilitator remained neutral in the discussion.

After the first two focus groups concluded, the facilitator needed to transcribe the recordings and collate with the notes to understand the discussions that had taken place and develop the secondary questions for focus group Three. Finally, the facilitator analyzed the discussion from focus group Three to formulate the final results.

Analysis of Results

Following all the focus group sessions, a process was required to sift and understand what the focus group members said through the transcribed discussions, and how this applied to the research question.

All three focus groups followed the same pattern of analysis. What was of primary concern was capturing the discussions that took place by transcribing all of the discussion. The method of analysis was to read the transcribed information from all three focus groups, and to then look for key phrases and themes that emerged. Sometimes this was consistent through all three focus groups and sometimes there were variances.

For this study, the transcribed information paired with the research question provided the conclusions that could be drawn. A method known as scissor and sort technique was used (Stewart, Shamdasani and Rook, 2007, pg 116). This refers to a process of identifying the parts of the discussion that apply to the research question and separating those from the overall discussions and focusing the analysis on those parts. The method used to do the scissor and sort technique was to shade in the relevant parts that were to be drawn out from the transcribed text. To secure some consistency with this technique, the co-facilitator also went through the text independently and then the facilitator and co-facilitator discussed the results together.

A further method of analysis to support the understanding of the transcribed information was content analysis and more specifically sign vehicle analysis. All three focus groups provided key words that emerged from the transcription and, by going through the discussions, the key words led to key themes, which then led to key discussions that could be analyzed.

Going into the analysis phase, and working with inductive research, it was important to let the transcribed information reveal the results. Using the scissor and sort method, combined with the sign vehicle analysis, an understanding of the focus group results could be applied to the research question. The advantage of inductive research is that it allows a journey of discovery since the results provide the direction that focuses on the research question.

Limitations and Biases of the Study

A limitation of this study was a consideration that the goal of this research was to understand what influences students to become leaders and not to examine the socio/economic or cultural results that might emerge through focus group discussion. It is important to note that in this study, any social/economic/cultural factors that might emerge were to be examined to the extent that they were understood to influence the students to get engaged in leadership opportunities. They were not to be examined in depth to comprehend their implications for the understanding of leadership in Indian or Asian culture and society. Those results may be reserved for examination in future research.

A further bias to consider was that as I am the Student Affairs Officer, most of the students who wanted to participate in the study were already known to me. They wanted to provide their insight and a potential issue might have been that the students would provide the answers that I was looking for rather than allowing open and unfiltered discussion to occur.

To balance this, at the outset of each focus group session, it was outlined that the purpose for the students being there was to understand their influences and to provide their insight on the questions asked. From reviewing the transcribed information from all the focus groups and the independent responses, it seems that the discussion was consistent with the questions asked.

Personal Reflections on Methodology

Going through the process of setting up and conducting three focus groups was rewarding since it provided opinions and impressions from the audience that this most impacts, the students. I might have my own opinions but hearing from the source did provide some insight of which I was not aware.

I believe the process undertaken in the methodology was a viable approach because it was important to create a control group and a specific group to determine if there were variances and to follow this up with deeper questions for focus group Three. Undertaking this method allowed variances, similarities and how they might apply to students and their influences to be considered. I would repeat the process of using two initial focus groups and maybe consider a gender application where one group is made up of males and the other females, or this could also be repeated using a first year student mix, with the other group being fourth year students. A third focus group for either scenario would involve a combined mix of the respective groups depending on whether gender or year of study criteria was used.

I believe timing is critical with regard to the conducting of focus groups. If I were to do the focus group sessions over again, there are a couple of approaches I would include, over and above email and Facebook. I would put a request out to faculty to address their class for five minutes to explain the study being undertaken. Targeting a few selected classes, there would be a greater chance of attracting students who might not normally participate because instead of just an email request, there is an immediate, personal invitation.

I believe that I would have asked the same questions if there was a need to do this a second time. I feel the process I followed, stemming from the students' personal understanding of leadership, combined with the influences on them, and followed by consideration of the university environment, led to a flow that was conducive to discussions of the topic of student leadership development.

The study looked at leadership, influences and engagement purely from a student perspective. A future study might examine these factors from a university or administrative level to see if the conditions presented in this research are consistent with those of the university.

In the future, it might be worth conducting the study outside SFU so that the students involved would have limited understanding of who I am and how I am involved in student leadership development. There might be a challenge of getting enough students since the use of email and Facebook would be limited outside SFU.

Summary

If a study involves student leadership development, then it makes sense to involve students in the process. For this study, the use of focus groups provided the medium for this. To ensure quality of research, three separate focus groups were conducted and the outline for this process centred on the structure of the focus groups, the selection of the students, formulation of the questions, the role of the facilitator and the analysis process. Through discussion and dialogue, an understanding of student leadership influences emerged that

will be discussed in the following chapter.

Chapter 4 – Presentation of Results
Process Initiated

One can read about leadership development and come up with intricate methodology to test the process. It is only through the use of a medium such as focus groups that the pure interaction of students that can direct research occurs. One could have anticipated the results from existing perceptions, experience or beliefs, but once the discussions were initiated, the interactions allowed a flow to occur that started establishing the basis for the study, and it became a journey through students' personal reflections and thoughts providing results concerning what influences them to get involved or not, with an emphasis on a collaborative environment based on relationships.

Going through the design of the focus group process, which involved having the questions arranged in advance, students selected and the time line in place, allowed for the organized delivery of each session. Being prepared as facilitator, I was able avoid focusing on the process and was free to concentrate on the group interactions, discussions and the physical actions (body language) of the participants.

Overview of Focus Groups

Focus Group Details

All three focus group sessions were unique in certain ways and were very similar in others. They each had their own identity emerge as students were answering the questions. What emerged, based on the results, was a constant theme of collaboration and relational leadership. At times, this was directly addressed in the discussion and, at other times, points were brought up that related to collaboration and relational leadership. There were also two sides to the discussion. One area was the collaborative needs of the students in their leadership development and the other was an examination by focus group members of the collaboration required at the university level to foster an environment of engagement.

Considering more areas that emerged, focus group One concentrated on 'textbook' and general concepts of leadership, while focus group Two placed emphasis on the external family environment as an influence. The discussion among focus group One used words like 'empowerment', 'passion' and 'direction' and expanded on these to talk about leadership as a process. Focus group Two talked about these ideas and concepts, too, but also incorporated more emphasis on the self and giving back to the community, involving ideas of servant leadership, family values, and cultural implications.

It seemed that focus group Three synthesized the two previous focus groups to talk about how they see the classroom structure as individualistic and extracurricular activities as more collaborative, as will be discussed. Focus group Three had difficulty linking work in the classroom to external leadership development in the community. There is a balance in the university setting that allows one to have an individualistic competitive nature and at the same time to be involved and engaged in campus activities that benefit others. It appeared that focus group Three was a hybrid of the two other focus groups. Their view of the classroom was of a person being an individual and pursuing grades. It was only outside the classroom that they felt part of a larger team or community, and higher-level goals emerged.

Focus Group Mechanics

Ideally, a focus group should have between six and twelve members. For the first focus group, twelve participants attended the session, and this became eleven as one participant volunteered to become a recorder. Focus group Two was initially made up of Indo-Canadians but, as we got closer to conducting the session, it appeared that having a sufficient number of Indo-Canadian participants would be a challenge, so the scope was widened to include any students with Asian roots. As a result, there were a total of seven members of focus group Two, which was composed of six Indo-Canadian students and one student of Chinese descent. Finally, focus group Three was a combination of nine students who fit the profile of focus groups One and Two, and who had not participated in a previous focus group.

The ideal way of selecting the focus group participants would be to have a significant number of pre-screening forms from which to choose the participants and to then use the demographics of the university to come up with an accurate formation of the focus groups. The provincial study by the Ministry of Advanced Education and Labour Market Development for British Columbia – Post Secondary Central Data Warehouse Standard Reports – Gender for 2008 (Ministry of Advanced Education, May 2008, pg 3) indicated a breakdown of 47% male to 53% female. See Appendix A Table 9 for the established provincial breakdown versus what the actual composition of the various focus groups.

Issues and Concerns

A limitation of this study is the possible gender imbalance noted and its potential influence on the outcome of the study. While the focus groups were skewed more heavily towards males compared to the standard distribution, where females slightly outnumber males, the gender imbalance had little apparent impact on the discussion as all students brought their personal views, experiences and understanding of leadership to the discussion.

A related concern raised for all three focus groups was that most of the participants were declared business students. The ideal mix would have been students from all faculties so that they were representative of the university demographics. While this might seem to be an issue, an aspect to consider is that Simon Fraser University has a unique situation; it is a school that promotes inter-disciplinary studies, so most of the students who attended the focus group sessions were declared business majors with an alternate faculty, or they were outright from another faculty. (See Appendix A Table 10)

A further issue identified was the aspect of the students knowing me personally and whether this would influence what they would say in response to the questions. I would argue that, because all of the students knew me, rather than this being a serious bias, it was advantageous to the focus group process as it allowed them to be more comfortable and open. If the facilitator were unknown to the group members, there would have been a longer period of building trust within the group.

A final concern was that, due to the time of the school year, the delay of the ethics review and other contributing factors, the mix of the students selected for the focus group sessions did not match the ideal mix as identified in Chapter Three. Given the focus groups actually used and the results obtained, similar results would likely have been attained had the original mix of focus group participants been used because, as mentioned earlier, the students were all fully engaged in the discussions. The use of independent responses became necessary to validate the results observed and recorded in the focus groups to ensure that the results were representative of the wider population. In a future study, it would be interesting to attempt to replicate these results using focus groups more representative of the population mix of the university.

Outcome of Results Based on Questions Posed

There are two areas of results that can be examined. One centres on the students and their projection outwards, towards student engagement and involvement. The other is the culture and environment created by the university that can foster or hinder student leadership development. The results from the focus groups provided a discovery of what mattered to the students when they reflected on their own personal experience and applied it to the discussions that took place.

Value of a Mission Statement

The foundation of creating a collaborative environment rests on understanding the values and mission of the organization. There has to be a common base in order for people to relate. This must align to individuals' personal values in order for them to have ownership and engagement. This also applies to university students.

> Your core value is set by the environment and you are then attracted to others that hold similar core values/mission.
>
> (Focus group Two, pg 3)

If the student feels that the values and mission align with their own, there is a much greater likelihood that the student will get involved. This is what the students would like to know or have an idea of before they undertake a project. In the follow up session, the question was posed to students of whether a mission statement or a vision mattered to them when selecting a project and whether it influenced their level of engagement. The results indicated:

> If there's a project and I have a clear vision and I am passionate then yes, I'll take a leadership role...It's important how a project relates to someone personally. If you don't have a clear vision, then difficult to do anything.
>
> (Focus group Three, pg 2)

As indicated by the students, values and a mission statement become the catalyst for a person to get involved. They form the foundation that collaboration and relationships emerge from because they facilitate the bringing together of people with a common interest.

Academic Studies and Leadership Development

One of the most significant outcomes of focus group Three arose from a question that asked about their academic experience and how they saw this complementing their leadership development. It was quite surprising that students indicated that, for the most part, they did not see the academic courses as having an influence on their leadership development. They saw academic education in this way:

> "To be involved, classes are actually an inconvenience, it's a hassle – I don't learn anything in class that I then say I will have to try and implement."
>
> (Focus group Three, pg 4)

> "We have to be here already, so gives us a facility to meet – class is there and we are here for classes but can do the engagement stuff as a result of being here."
>
> (Focus group Three, pg 4)

There is a need to explore this idea further because universities are in place to provide academic and personal development opportunities and, if the students do not recognize the connection, there is a need to see where this connection fails.

Students saw the classroom environment as being all about getting a good grade, while community service and involvement are more about a commitment made and finishing a project. One member of focus group three said:

> Classes hurt because it makes you competitive.

(Focus group Three, pg 4)

There is a lack of collaboration and relationships when a student is in the classroom setting. The environment provides an individualist feel to the classroom as the students compete with each other for marks. What the students in focus group three outlined further was that there are courses that are a necessity while they work towards their degree that are not in line with their natural tendencies and, as discussed earlier, this helps to promote their involvement in projects. It is when students align courses that are of interest to them with their own preferences for personal development that they can benefit from the influences pushing them to get involved. For the students in the focus groups, experiences outside the classroom were more important than what they received as a mark. One student said:

> When you are in your 40's or 50's, it really won't matter what you got on an econ course. You leave your mark by getting involved, not by getting good grades.

(Focus group Three, pg 6)

Situational Leadership

Another aspect that came up quite often in all the focus group sessions was leadership based on situations that were presented to students. There are implications for collaboration and relationships in this instance because the group dynamics outlined become the ingredients for student engagement. It creates a situation that sparks the interest of the student. According to focus, group One:

> I find in work, there is limited opportunity to be a leader but in school, there is the opportunity to be more flexible and the environment dictates the situation and the role of the leader.
>
> (Focus group One, pg 2)

From the students' perspective, they see the need to apply the situation to their personal leadership involvement and engagement, according to a person's strengths and weaknesses. If people feel comfortable in a role, and the need matches that role, depending on the values and mission, they will assume the leadership position or get involved as followers.

Related to the concept of situation was the idea of ambiguity, which came up in focus groups One and Three. Ambiguity is what creates a situation in which students will decide to get involved or not. While some students thrive on ambiguity, others may shy away from it. Ambiguity, according to focus group One,

> …is about being in a situation that you don't know a lot about and this can make it difficult to become a leader off the bat. Taking a leadership role becomes much more difficult because you might lack experience – but if you have the core values that are transferable, you might be able to take on the role.
>
> (Focus group One, pg 6)

What the students in focus group One brought up was that they learn to identify the strengths and weaknesses of the team members and the leadership role moves from one person to another, based on the experience that each person brings to the team. In other words, leadership to them is fluid and it becomes an influence on whether they get involved or not. This becomes the cornerstone of situational leadership and ambiguity. Through experience, the student learns to accept the ambiguous nature of the setting but this can only be accomplished in a collaborative setting. Experiencing ambiguity by oneself is not as appealing as experiencing ambiguity within a group.

Leadership as a Process

All three focus groups commented on and provided examples of how they see leadership as a process and not just an activity that one does. The process involves those around you and the act of following, which involves the relationships and collaboration that emerge through interactions. The groups understood that there is a process, which was stated as:

1) Leading – the person and their capacity to lead a group of followers
2) Situation – the environment and the state of affairs that provide the opportunities or not for someone to get involved
3) Completion of the project – where there is a goal outlined that the leader and group work towards

(Focus group One, pg 1)

This was significant because they see leadership and influence as going beyond the sole leader and encompassing the idea of leading as a movement. The situation presented indicates the type of leader to emerge, based on what is occurring. Finally, there is completion, where there is a definite conclusion to the initiative. All three of these conditions need to be in place for influences to take effect and others to follow suit. This can be expanded the following way:

> We view leadership as a relational process of people together attempting to accomplish change or make a difference to benefit the common good.
>
> (Komives, Lucas and McMahon, 1998, pg 68)

This quote reinforces what our students said earlier about their view that leadership is a process that works to the common good with its foundation being a process.

Taking the aspect of process further, it would appear that the students in the focus groups saw their entire university experience as a whole, and that it was a process, which involved transformation. This transitioned from the academic experience to self-serving motivation, and finally to working to benefit the community. It was suggested that, once the student is engaged, that they start to realize the greater benefit of being involved and their mindset shifts from one that is self-serving to one that focuses on working on community engagement projects.

> At first, it was self-serving to start out because I did not know how or what it would lead to, and then I took projects on for better good and realized that there is a benefit to getting involved.
>
> (Focus group One, pg 3)

The focus group members seemed to suggest that there is a progression of involvement:

- 1st year student - engaged in academics because they are getting used to the academic nature of the campus

- 2nd and 3rd year - students are now discovering things that are available on campus; however, the need to get involved is more on the self-serving nature

- 3rd and 4th year students - in tune with engagement and are now involved because they see the needs in the community and want to give back. It is a realization that it is more than marks

> (Focus group Three, pg 4)

This was an interesting observation regarding the progression of students from a developmental perspective. It involves the maturing of the student, and a progression from an individualistic state to one that establishes relationships and functions in a more collaborative environment.

Barriers to Student Leadership Development

Considering influences on getting involved, there is an emphasis on the collaboration and relationships that emerge while students transform during their university experience. Barriers, on the other hand, depend more on the individuals and their personal situations.

Time and Funding

It was quite evident from focus group One that one of the most significant reasons a student would not get involved related to the simple aspects of time and funding. Students who are paying their own tuition find that they do not have the necessary time, because of their need for funding and having to work full-time.

> Time, value and priority in your life = things in your life make the decisions for you.
>
> (Focus group One, pg 3)

What this means is that if a student has to pay rent or tuition, this would take priority over other social and involvement aspects. This becomes a considerable barrier to engagement. The student might want to be involved, but priority of work and commitments outside university might dictate that they are not able to.

Cultural

While focus group One spoke about time and financial barriers, which were quite specific to the individual, for focus group Two, it was more about culture and the wider community. It is possible to focus on the culture and sense of community in an organization like a university, or culture could be taken to mean the personal aspect of an individual that reflects on external influences such as their own personal cultural/family identity. These are different concepts but equally important to someone of a multicultural background.

For this study, we examined examples of both self and the university community culture based on the discussions that emerged from the three focus groups. Focus group One did not really bring any form of the social aspects of culture forward in their discussions while focus group Two spoke at length about being from a different culture and the impact that their parents have on their getting involved in activities outside the classroom.

Taking this to the individual level, our students interact in the university culture but they also bring their own cultural identities and values to the university. As noted by focus group Two, this can be a challenge at times with students of immigrant parents. The parents impose their ideals on the students and this at times works counter to what the student would like to do.

> Being the youngest in the family and a female Indo-Canadian born in Canada, there is an expectation to behave in a certain way. There is control exerted by my parents to not get involved. When I am in university, I can now exert control or involvement, which is not available when I am outside of the institution and in my cultural setting.
>
> (Focus group Two, pg 4)

It is when they are on campus that they feel that they are empowered to get involved and engaged. A further discussion took place where students felt that they had to push back against their parents and make them understand that what they are doing at the university is worthwhile:

> Need to show parents that it is more than good marks. It is not just partying and fun and games…you are actually learning and applying your knowledge outside the classroom.
>
> (Focus group Two, pg 5)

According to students in focus group Two, they did not feel marginalized because of their culture, as outlined by Lin in the literature review, when they entered university; it is more about the pressure they are under from their parents who do not understand the concept of engagement. This does change over time if the parents start seeing how it positively influences their children:

> At first there was pressure but after a while they see how student has changed and that they are not doing it because it is just fun.
>
> (Focus group Two, pg 6)

While most of the interactions of focus group Two brought up challenges to engagement based on their personal cultural situations, there are instances where the student does embody their culture and this does help strengthen influences to get involved in other capacities:

> The influence to get involved comes from many factors. A lot of the organizations that I've volunteered for deal with issues in my culture and that is one of the major reasons why I volunteer.
>
> (Independent Responses, pg 8)

This last point demonstrates that personal cultural implications are not all bad. At times, they can play an important role in engagement when students reflect on their upbringing and if it was instilled at the family and friends level, matching their value system and in an environment that is collaborative based on their own needs.

Administration and Faculty

It was brought up by all focus groups and in the independent responses that the university administration needs to get out more and "feel the pulse" of the student population. The perception of many of the participants was that the grassroots administrative level provides programs and initiatives that foster student engagement, leadership and collaboration; however, at the level of the President, Vice Presidents and Directors things become hierarchal, bureaucratic and lack a collaborative spirit.

> Universities can listen to their students; listen to their needs and show them the results of their ideas so they can feel like they are making a difference.
>
> (Independent responses pg 8)

This reinforces the need to have relationships and dialogue between the university administration and the students, because the students need to know what their university stands for, and how it matches their values. There was a sense that students feel that the

59

university works in silos and is out for the self-interest of the particular group. When asked about the university as a whole and engagement:

> More structure – commonality and the key is building on the relationships establishes a foundation.
>
> (Focus group One, pg 9)

Note that, in this situation, they are not calling for more bureaucracy, but rather an environment that promotes collaboration and shared goals.

Faculty Engagement

The perception of the students in the focus groups is that there is a lack of faculty involvement and that this is connected to faculty performance evaluations. There is no incentive for the faculty to be engaged and then inspire students to get involved.

> Work it into their performance evaluations – no real hard incentives for faculty to get involved…there is nothing tangible.
>
> (Focus group Three, pg 11)

The students of focus group Two suggested that the professors have considerable influence with students and, if they encourage students to get involved with a project or initiative, the students generally will. Faculty members are in a unique position because they have the capacity to build a collaborative environment, since they wield a considerable amount of influence over the students. The students look up to the faculty as mentors, teachers and people who have experience that they can share. From this trust and relationships that can benefit students' leadership development can be built.

Observations

Focus groups involve the interaction of people while they discuss issues that are posed to them and become the ethnography component of the study. While the content of the discussion is of primary value, physical observation of the group adds a dimension to the analysis.

> Qualitative observation depends less on available instruments and more on the evaluator or observer.
>
> (Worthen and Sanders, 1987, pg 309)

Observation is critical because it allows one to note things that might not be picked up from the transcript and interpretations can change depending on observable behaviours in focus groups.

> Not to sit and label every time I see something but rather have an understanding how it fits into the situation and if it is the best form of leadership in the circumstance and combinations of styles of leadership.
>
> (Learning Log – Phase 3, Activity 3)

Observation complements the verbal interaction that occurs, so that a full process of assessment is available. Considering this, some notable points arose out of observing the participants of the three focus groups.

There were a couple of participants in each of the focus groups who appeared to be dominating the discussions. They would sit upright and every so often lean forward into the discussion; however, it is worth mentioning that all members, whether involved or quietly participating in the discussion, had something to contribute. An observation of the quiet individuals was that a few of them would rather sit back, take in the discussion and then have something profound to say. There was another group of quiet members who seemed to have an intrinsic quietness. It would appear that focus groups One and Three had individual members who stood out more, while focus group Two seemed more balanced in terms of discussion.

Group Two participants seemed to be a bit more respectful of other members because it seemed that, in focus groups, One and Three, students would be more apt to cut each other off to get their point in, but in focus group Two, they would first sit and listen, and then contribute.

It appeared that the group members were balanced in choosing their seating arrangement, which was random. Some members did seem to know each other and they spent time chatting but, when it came down to discussion, they were focused on the task at hand.

All three focus groups seemed shy or reserved when it came to talking about their own personal accomplishments. When asked, they seemed to laugh a little about it or look away from the other members when they spoke. It appeared that most of the members were modest about their own accomplishments, but when they were talking in general terms, they had no problem expressing their opinions.

On certain occasions when asked about how their academic learning and their leadership development complement each other, or when students of focus group Two started to talk about their personal influences in relation to family or culture, the discussion turned more to personal reflection. The tone changed from regular discussion to almost a sense of frustration in which either the university or their parents did not 'get it' or understand why they are involved.

Members of all three focus groups seemed to feel free to talk to each other during a break and after the session. It was obvious not all the focus group members knew each other; however, they were comfortable enough to approach, shake hands and start talking about their academic experiences.

Finally, as a functional observation of the number of participants in each focus group, it did seem that, in focus group One, with eleven participants, it was far more difficult to get involved discussions going because each participant wanted to contribute. The seven members of focus group Two provided an opportunity to have more involved discussions on the topics. With nine members of focus group Three, discussion was still manageable and provided an environment where all members were able to get their point across. Based on this observation of focus group members, the ideal number would be between seven and nine members.

Summary

Literature review and a process of undertaking a research methodology can provide a structure to answer questions; however, the interaction and discussion of a focus group provide a comparative tool to balance the investigation. Focus group interactions in this case revealed that collaboration and relational leadership are important when considering influences such as a value/mission statement, situational leadership, culture and other commitments. Focus group interaction provides a mechanism to test out the theory with real live discussion. Sometimes this reinforces initial thoughts and sometimes it can provide unexpected revelations.

Chapter 5 – Discussion of Results

Some significant findings emerged through the use of focus groups. Taking the established literature review and applying the knowledge gained from structured interactions of focus groups provided insights on a number of fronts. Important findings involved how collaboration and relational leadership tie in to student engagement and development. As will be examined, collaboration and relational leadership influence the students' pursuit of leadership engagement and there is a need for the university to become more collaborative so that an environment that fosters student leadership development can emerge.

Collaboration

It would appear that one fundamental aspect of improving student engagement, which was evident in the focus group discussions as well as the literature, is a need to have an environment of collaboration. This was outlined by the Kellogg Foundation:

> Furthermore, since the concepts of "leadership" and "leader" imply that there are other people involved; leadership is, by definition, a collective or group process.

> (Kellogg Foundation, 2000, pg 8)

What is important about this concept is that it moves thinking about the traditional leadership view outlined in Chapter Two, about the leader as the sole authority, to a view of participatory leadership, which embodies the empowering of followers into the leadership process.

Through all three focus groups, one of the emerging themes on influences focused on providing an environment of collaboration. This included a macro view of the university as an institution that can work towards a collaborative community that allows an environment to thrive in which students have a foundation encouraging to student leadership development. From a micro perspective, the students, from an individual point of view, discussed the need to work in a collaborative setting outside the classroom. If the university campus has a collaborative culture, then it permeates into the classroom, administration and other areas. Based on the research, it is the responsibility of the university to provide an environment that engages students in getting involved.

In the current trend of leadership development in post-secondary institutions, leadership should be more about the collective group rather than the individual.

> Leadership in the new millennium will be much more collaborative and therefore should encourage consensus, cooperation, and collaboration instead of competition and conflict.
>
> (Brungardt, 1998, pg 5)

Taking this thought further, an aspect of the focus groups is highlighted in which the students feel that the classroom environment is one of competition and not collaboration. Outside the classroom, collaboration can take place, but what is needed is a shift of the focus in the classroom, to creating a structure where the students can work together, which will have an impact on their personal leadership development.

Relational Leadership

Another aspect that emerged from the student focus groups was the importance of relationship building and how it influences the students becoming involved.

> I am inspired to get involved by motivation to make a difference. I feel that my contribution to organizations and volunteer work helps others reach their goals and awards me the satisfaction of making a difference in other people's lives.
>
> (Independent responses, pg 5)

This concept is linked to collaboration because, in order to have collaboration, there need to be relationships. It is about the interactions between people. In Chapter Two there was a reference to relational leadership, which embodies the five principles of being inclusive, empowering, purposeful, ethical and process-orientated. (Komives, Lucas, McMahon, 1998, pg, 22) These aspects become the foundation for establishing relationships and a base from which to collaborate.

> Thus, leadership is not the work of a single person; rather it can be explained and defined as a "collaborative endeavour", among group members.
>
> (Brungardt C. L, 1998, pg 2)

What needs to be understood is that students bring varying degrees of engagement and relationships. While they might build strong partnerships in one instance, they might be a follower or less involved in another. The aspect of relationships might be found in academic learning, work, the community etc. Relational leadership is a dynamic process that shifts, depending on the needs and context of the student. In other words as situations change, relationships are drawn upon and the role of the leader may be shared amongst the group members as the need arises.

> The leader needs to recognize who has the strength among the group and not be threatened by the strength...leader also needs to know when to follow.
>
> (Focus group One, pg 1)

> Personal connections – if there is no personal connection, then I won't get involved.
>
> (Focus group One, pg 4)

This can influence the extent to which a student becomes engaged or is influenced to be involved.

The relationships that a student establishes become a catalyst that provides opportunities that a student chooses to pursue or not.

Influences

Student and University

In chapter two, social identity was discussed. The idea is that students need to look beyond just themselves and to focus more on their group dynamics. (Buchanan and Huczynski, 2004, pg 355) It is important to understand that the group is greater than the single student. Therefore, when students speak about the environment outside the classroom, they are speaking directly about social identity. Social identity is significant because it provides an avenue for the student to be a part of a collaborative effort. The concern, though, is that students have multiple involvements and not just one source of influence. There is a need to understand the impact that social issues, academic studies, personal lives and so on have on the engagement that the student pursues.

Student Commitments Outside the Classroom

As mentioned, what came up in the discussion was that students do not view their lives and experiences as a one-dimensional model solely based in the classroom, but rather they see unavoidable influences based on situations, people around them and context, and, as a result, different leadership and followership positions may apply and the university needs to understand this. For example, in focus group One and Three, it was brought up that:

> Time, value and priority in your life determine your engagement.
>
> (Focus group One, pg 3)

> People have niches in places other than SFU. They might be leaders in different opportunities; they might have stuff going on elsewhere.
>
> (Focus group Three, pg 12)

What this implies is that students have to make decisions on what they can do based on what is occurring in their lives. This also expands to three aspects of their lives while they are students: school (class, exams, and papers), external life (friends, work and volunteer commitments) and personal life (family, culture, personal development).

> There is a finite amount of things I can do. I only have so much energy and time to go around. If school is a priority, then I am dedicated there, then when that is over, I can concentrate on the other aspects of my life.
>
> (Focus group One, pg 6)

It was suggested that when students are in class or doing final exams, all other priorities seem to diminish temporarily. When they are on a break between semesters or taking a semester off to work, then their school commitment is minimal. This may be illustrated using a Venn Diagrams, indicating that the commitment of a student is constantly changing depending on the immediate situation. (See Appendix B Figure 3 and Figure 4)

These diagrams provide a view of how priorities for students shift and change based on what is occurring. From an individual student level, there is overlap between the school, external and personal areas.

Student Leadership Influences

It is in the best interest of the university to provide opportunities for students to get involved in any number of on-campus and off-campus projects. As noted throughout, there is a responsibility, beyond academic studies, that the university is entrusted with. There is also the practical intelligence that occurs in conjunction with academic intelligence. If a university is proactive and builds a collaborative environment based on solid relationships, then positive influences emerge that will engage students.

Situational Leadership

All focus groups talked about the situation presented, which created opportunities for the students to find the initiative to be engaged and build on their experience. According to discussion among the focus groups and the Hersey-Blanchard model outlined in Chapter Two, the level of ambiguity of a project creates a situation, which determines the level of leadership and involvement of students. The learning environment in a university is based on creating some ambiguity in class projects because students need to figure out solutions to academic questions. From the students' perspective, as outlined in the results section, the focus group members saw leadership as a three step process:

1) The process of leading
2) The leader emerging based on the situation at hand
3) That there is a completion to the project

(Focus group One, pg 1)

Drawing these three points together with the concept of ambiguity provides the students with a gauge of what the level of leadership behaviour should be. Collaboration and relationships help, by sharing experience and work, to soften the degree of ambiguity and provide a more balanced approach to solving problems and working on projects. If there is a high level of ambiguity, the inclination is for the leader to provide a more 'telling', or 'directed', environment to the group and this is usually in consultation with a university administrator. If there is a lower level of ambiguity, then there is a progression which provides a more 'delegating' and 'participatory' process, involving limited participation of a faculty member or administrator. From a student affairs perspective, the level of comfort and frequency of past projects determines whether the university administration should intervene to help if difficulties arise. Since collaboration and relational leadership provide a more stable situation, responsibilities are shared and there is more opportunity to provide an environment that encourages engagement.

Self-serving Transformation to Engagement

Influence on students to become involved in a leadership role can be as micro-focused as a self-serving objective, or macro-focused while working towards a noble goal. A significant concept that came up was the idea that students start out in a self-serving mode and that this can transform once they get involved in a cause that is based more on giving back to the community. It was outlined how this starts from an internalizing process and slowly transforms into the outward projection of community engagement.

The influence on students undertaking a project for self-serving needs is based on how it directly affects them. An example of self-serving motivation is getting involved in a club because it is felt that it will look good on a resume. This is still an influence, even though it is based on self-serving needs, because it does get the student involved. It may be this initial involvement, which unintentionally begins the transformational process leading to the individual pursing a project for the better good of the community. This can be linked to the Kellogg foundation and the idea of transformative leadership.

> We believe that leadership is a process that is ultimately concerned with fostering change…directed toward some future end or condition which is desired or valued.
>
> (Kellogg Foundation, 2000, pg 8)

The Kellogg Foundation views this as an important concept in promoting student engagement. Transformative change varies depending on each person's own particular circumstances and development.

Servant Leadership

While focus group One discussed the aspects of self-serving leadership that transformed motivations into something more noble, focus group Two talked more about servant leadership and servanthood. What was brought up in focus group Two is that to lead, a person must demonstrate servant leadership.

> The leader is not there for the glamour of it. They are involved by passion about a cause and are willing to sacrifice. It is about leading by example.
>
> (Focus group Two, pg 2)

Within a university setting, there needs to be just a spark from a few dedicated individuals who exert their influence and initiative in a university project that becomes a catalyst for others.

> The key component here is the uplifting and empowering of the citizen to take control of their own community and bring about positive social change. People motivate and empower each other.
>
> (Grizzell B, 2008, pg 4)

Usually with servanthood, the influence for students is modelling. As Kouzes and Posner outline, 'model the way' is an important influence in getting other people involved and engaged. The reason it influences others to get involved is that they see the 'feel good factor' in doing so, and also how it can benefit others.

Influences on Students Not Getting Involved

While there are opportunities and situations created that provide an environment of engagement, there are also instances mentioned by students during the focus groups that result in students not being involved. What is interesting is that the influences that get students involved are more a matter of choice whereas the environment being less flexible often dictates those influences that create non-involvement.

Time and Funding

It was consistent among members of all three focus group that a central reason why an individual might not get involved is based on two valuable resources – time and the need for funds. If students are independent and paying for their tuition, housing and expenses, then there is not a lot of time available for them to get involved in campus activities or community projects. Their time is dedicated more towards gaining practical experience. It is worth mentioning that, while this does not directly impact the notion of giving back or community involvement, it does still address one of the foundations of involvement outside the classroom, because it directly involves the individual's journey to gain practical experience and this can foster the development of their personal leadership through the relationships they establish outside the university. It is important to remember that leadership development embodies both academic studies and practical experience. Students are not able to directly contribute to the university or be as involved in the community as they would like to because they have to meet their own basic needs; however, gaining external experience does benefit students on campus when they become engaged with a working student because it draws realism into the formula, as working students can share their experiences.

To demonstrate the extent that work is a critical consideration on student engagement, the Fall 2007 Undergraduate Student Survey examined a number of factors on student life, one of which was work. In this study, 71% of the SFU respondents are actively working. (Simon Fraser University – Undergraduate Survey, Fall 2007, pg 53) This reinforces the idea that a large portion of students might find it difficult to be fully engaged in a leadership capacity. (See Appendix A Table 11)

Cultural Implications

Focus group Two, being a multi-cultural group, raised another concern regarding an influence that may result in students not getting involved. The parents of these students feel that involvement in extra-curricular programs interferes with their main idea of why students are in university, which is to get an education. From focus group Two, it would appear that the perceived traditional cultural implications are that one goes to university to get an education and then transition into a job. Doing volunteer work or participating in a club is not seen as directly contributing towards students' personal development. This cultural implication actually puts the students in a very difficult situation because on the one hand, North American post-secondary Student Affairs Offices provide opportunities to undertake co-curricular activities and would like students to develop their personal and professional development outside the classroom. On the other hand, students are facing a dilemma because their socio/economic and cultural upbringing is suggesting that they should not be involved because it is a waste of time.

> I don't tell my parents everything I do because they won't understand. I might tell them what I am doing but not why.
>
> (Focus group Two, pg 5)

The students in focus group Two talked about how frustrating this is because often they cannot tell their parents that they are actively involved and making a difference in the community.

Commuter Campus

Another reason for students not getting involved is that they feel the campus is a commuter campus and that they do not want to spend more time in a place that consumes so much of their energy and time.

SFU has a commuter campus mentality. As a result, people focus more on their lives outside of the university and don't realize the opportunities on campus.

(Focus group Three, pg 13)

They have a social life outside university and choose to keep the two separate. In this instance, while students might not be involved on-campus activities, they might still be engaged off campus in community projects with a different group of individuals not associated with university such as family, friends, church or co-workers, to name a few. In this situation, students have priorities and commitments elsewhere, so they choose to get involved off campus.

The University Environment

As we have observed in literature, universities must shift from a purely academic educational environment to one that involves more social and personal development. There is a need to build on this experience because it fosters solid leadership development in the student. Zimmerman-Oster and Burkhardt examined thirty hallmarks, which identify successful programs in leadership development, two of which are worth considering here:

1) Successful programs include a comprehensive, coordinated educational strategy, which includes experiential learning opportunities and 2) Sustained programs involve not just individual skill development, but also capacity building for the institution and the community it serves.

(Zimmerman-Oster and Burkhardt, 1999, pg 59)

This outlines how there need to be more collaboration and relationships so that an environment of engagement can flourish.

Examining the university as a whole, it may seem that there is a bureaucratic and administrative foundation that is limiting and not too accommodating when considering collaboration. There are, however, certain programs and faculties that are incorporating leadership development within and outside the classroom. At SFU, when examining the business program, a number of students in the focus groups indicated that qualitative courses incorporating group projects and presentations go further towards developing leadership than the quantitative courses such as accounting and finance.

> Skills learned in class that are practical, like working together to develop a brochure in a marketing class for a club I am associated with has helped in my contribution to that club.
>
> (Focus group Three, page 5)

There was also a realization on a couple of fronts that academic classes create a competitive arena and that work in groups outside class promotes a more collaborative and engaging environment. A university has to realize that, while they are an establishment that is rich in tradition, there is a need to keep in mind that the students may have changed and that the current academic system is outdated. Examining the Generation Y audience today, it is evident that they put more emphasis on things outside what the university provides. In a recent survey by Brainstorm looking at Generation Y, universities across Canada, including SFU, were surveyed. (See Appendix F) There were 262 SFU Business respondents from a wider 4,568 across Canada total and when asked about what made them enrol.

> Get a good job was number one while get a good education was number four.
>
> (Brainstorm survey, 2008

What this indicated is that students are looking more towards gaining practical experience than academic success.

Flexibility versus Structure

Some aspects of a university education provide rigidity and some areas more flexibility. The recommendation from students in the focus groups was that some aspects of the students' education, as they enter university, should be structured in a semi-cohort format to manage the students' level of engagement. The reason for this is that, if you leave it in the hands of the students, there will be varying degrees of involvement. (Focus group One, pg 9)

> A cohort program is about having more structure in year one and two and is valuable to connect you with a core group of people.
>
> (Focus group One, pg 10)

The suggested semi-cohort model is not so rigid that the student has no choice and is forced to get involved; it is rather something that allows variety. An example is students interested in international issues; if they do not have international experience, then they only read about it. Instead of telling the students that they have to go away on exchange, one could recommend that the students try either the exchange, a 2-week international field school, an international co-op or an international conference. Through being offered variety, the students do not feel pressured to get involved and can choose the best experience. In the current system, students are left to discover projects on their own or through friends who have gotten involved, so the engagement is only as consistent as the relationships established by the student. From a personal level as the Student Affairs Officer, I see the merit in the semi-cohort model. At the present time, after the initial orientation, we leave it up to students to come to us, rather than instituting a semi-structured program that would enable us to monitor and assist their development and that would also foster a collaborative environment.

University Faculty Engagement

Collectively, the focus group members spoke about the importance and influence that administration and faculty members have on student engagement. The perception of focus group Three was that faculty is encouraged to do research and any involvement is 'off the side of the desk'. Related to this, there need to be incentives built in to the system that allows a faculty member to participate and engage students without being penalized.

> Professors create an impact and influence on the student and can drive a student to get involved on campus activities that complement the classroom.
>
> (Focus group Three, pg 12)

The perception of the students in the focus groups was that faculty members did not have a strong awareness of what was available and how getting the student involved could influence the individual students' personal development and leadership. Students look up to a faculty member as their coach and guide. There is a huge opportunity lost if this is not utilised to promote engagement of the student.

> The professor makes a connection in the classroom – they must get to know the student. My favourite professors are the ones I have gotten to know, they got to know me. The professor needs to be open to this sort of interaction.
>
> (Focus group Three, pg 12)

More and more, it is about creating a collaborative environment based on solid faculty relationships in which both administration and faculty need to work together in fostering leadership development programs. In a past learning log entry, it was stated:

> Better communication and teamwork between departments and faculties would result in less self interest and more shared successes. We have an environment that often overlaps and are mutually dependent upon each other.
>
> (Thiara, Learning Log, May 20, 2007)

Working together creates the strength of relationships that allows for change that can work to the benefit to the student.

Academic Studies and Practical Experience

Based on the findings of this study, it is apparent that a university exists to provide an environment of academic learning. This aspect is, however, only part of the development of the overall student. The post-secondary community fosters the transformation of an individual and this incorporates faculty, administration, and all the other areas of influence. It is rare to find a student who does not transform from one position of experience to another.

Understanding practical intelligence from the literature review is important because this is where the students apply knowledge gained from the classroom to their interpretation of the 'real world'. It was stated by focus group Three that they do not really derive measurable benefits to their leadership development by attending class; however, consideration of practical intelligence points to the fact that they do. Sternberg feels that this can apply in the following three situations:

- Changing one self to suit the environment (adaptation)
- Changing the environment to suit oneself (shaping)
- Finding a new environment within which to work (selection)

(Sternberg R. J, 2002, pg 355)

This concept can be taken further to demonstrate that its foundation is also based on transformational leadership. Students who enter post-secondary institution do so for their personal development, and a transformation occurs in their academic learning as they develop their analytical, decision making and communication skills. When they take this and apply it outside the classroom to a community or some extra-curricular project, they have applied their academic intelligence in a practical form. Therefore, when students say that they derive limited or no experience from the classroom related to their leadership development, this is not quite accurate, because what they learn in the classroom complements how they apply themselves externally to a project.

Transformational leadership was referenced earlier; it is seen as a prime aspect of the university because that is what they are in place for, to transform an individual's limited knowledge to extensive knowledge in a particular field.

Sometimes we separate the individual from the collective experience because they are viewed as parallel entities. In the focus groups, students indicated that what they do in the classroom is reflected in their own personal development but when they are working on a group project outside the class that is collective development. They see these two experiences as running side-by-side and not really intersecting.

The Kellogg Foundation indicated ten individual and group qualities of transformative leadership, which are:

Individual	Group
• Self knowledge	• Collaboration
• Authenticity	• Shared purpose
• Empathy	• Division of labour
• Commitment	• Disagreement with respect
• Competence	• Learning environment

(Kellogg Foundation, 2000, pg 14)

Overall, transformational leadership development is derived from both the individual and group. Adding to this concept, Kouzes and Posner (2002) examined over 17,000 business leaders and what they concluded is in line with the W.K. Kellogg Foundation. Kouzes and Posner came up with Five Practices of Exemplary Leadership, later expanded to include

Five Practices of Exemplary Student Leadership. The Five Principles did not change too much when it was focused on students. The following outlines these five points:

- Challenging the process
- Inspiring a shared vision
- Enabling others to act
- Modelling the way
- Encouraging the heart

(Kouzes and Posner, 2002, pg 13-20)

Combining the ten points of the Kellogg Foundation with the five points of student leadership of Kouzes and Posner establishes a foundation that a model such as Kotter's Eight Steps to Change can incorporate. The points outlined create an environment that builds on collaboration, in which the institution and all its stakeholders are working together for the benefit of the students.

What I Have Learned and Contribution to Knowledge

Going through the research and focus group process provided the foundation for comparison of the experience of the Student Affairs Office to the research. For me, the aspects of collaboration and relational leadership are the most important points to emerge from the study. The student engagement that I perform is a microcosm of how collaboration and relationships are enacted at a university. Incorporating the two models just outlined those of the Kellogg Foundation and Kouzes and Posner can provide an environment that fosters engagement and involvement of students who might not otherwise get involved. All of this complements what was discussed in the focus group sessions, looking at the personal development of student leadership through a collaborative and relational environment. What is valuable is that the principles outlined by the Kellogg

Foundation and by Kouzes and Posner are attainable with the resources available within the walls of a post-secondary establishment.

Concerning a contribution to knowledge, there is a unique circumstance at this point where there is literature combined with focus groups providing insight. A further dimension is the experience of the Student Affairs Office that can be applied. It provides a university, student and administrative view of what influences students to get involved or not. As stated earlier in the study, the Student Affairs position promotes student engagement and we have seen the progression to an unprecedented level of involvement; however, there was never a full understanding of the mechanics of how this position applies to engagement. Going through the study provides a foundation on which to base understanding of how SFU Business can incorporate further engagement, and how other universities might find parallels or opportunities to institute engagement possibilities for their students.

Summary

There are two concepts that are critical when talking about student engagement and influences collaboration and relational leadership. Each supports the other in providing an opportunity to create a rich environment that builds leadership development. The concepts become the foundation for examination of what influences students to get involved or not, and provide an idea of what a university must take into consideration when looking at leadership development. The institution and the individual student both need to be examined along with how they complement each other.

Chapter 6 – Conclusion

> Applying the principles of transformative leadership will help to create a genuine community of learners; environments where students, faculty, and administrators can benefit personally and contribute to the common good.
>
> (Kellogg Foundation, 2000, pg 87)

A University is more than classrooms and education. It is a community in itself, having the capacity to inspire those within its walls to go out and become agents of change. Students can choose to go through their education being passive bystanders to change or can engage themselves in a process that becomes change.

The research question for this study outlined what influences a student to get involved or not, and how the university could leverage those influences to provide opportunities for further engagement. The literature review provided views from various sources looking at leadership influences, and the position a university holds in the development of student leaders. Following this, the methodology section outlined how leadership is a social construct and how the primary research for this study was to use focus groups. The next chapter provided results elicited from students who participated in the focus groups, on what influenced them to get involved or not and how they viewed the university's position. Finally, a discussion of the results provided an opportunity to look at the focus group results in the light of the literature review, providing a forum to examine what all this meant. A number of key points emerged in response to the initial question on what influences or does not influence students in terms of leadership development and how the university might leverage these influences.

Motivation for Research

Working in a student affairs capacity, I am in a position to see both aspects of influences on student engagement. There is a need to bridge academic education more effectively with practical 'real life' application for students and, from a student's perspective, to provide an environment rich in opportunities to get students involved in making a difference.

As noted at the outset, there is a personal motivation for this research. When I attended and graduated from SFU, there were limited opportunities available to work towards my own personal leadership development. Now working as a Student Affairs Officer, incorporating 25+ years of industry experience, and conducting this study, I have identified a need to build on programs that engage students so they are looking beyond their transcripts.

Influences on Change

Collaboration and Relationships

Collaboration and relational leadership were discussed at length. These concepts go hand in hand. In order to initiate change, there must be strength in the relationships of all involved. These solid relationships provide a foundation that becomes the root of the change so that it is more widely adopted and accepted. The strength of relational leadership is its ability to adapt to change and create a situation in which a model such as Kotter's Eight Stage Process to Foster Change can be applied. What is imperative is that all the parties in a university environment must work towards this change and establish a solid relationship with those around them. From a student's perspective, if a model like Kotter's is instituted, it allows changes to occur that provide a richer environment for student engagement. This can happen when there is open communication about engagement, support to foster this engagement and an understanding of what these influences mean to the student and the community at large.

Overcoming a Disconnect

Regarding the results of the focus groups and the reflection on the literature, one of the underlying aspects to consider is an overall disconnect. There is a disconnect between the university and their students, and between the students and their academic journey. Results demonstrate that the universities carry on a continuum of curriculum development, research and rankings as they have always done. The fact is that universities have remained unchanged, not aligning with how students have emerged and developed from the Baby Boomers, through Generation X to Generation Y, and now the Millennial student. There are components and departments of the university that have made strides, such as business schools and student development on campus, and that lead the way, but there is a limited focus on creating a collaborative environment that is built on a foundation of relationships.

Turning now to the student, there is a disconnect between the student and their institution. If students feel that their academic education does not complement their leadership development, then they are misguided. Their leadership development is composed of all the forces that are around them. This incorporates their academic education, social life, work, sport, and so on. Their academic education is one component of their development and can be seen as their leadership education, which factors into their overall leadership development. Therefore, even though they are doing a course that they perceive as not related to leadership development, there are still transferable skills to be derived from academic education. In order to overcome the disconnect, there is a need to change the focus and environment of the university, and also the perception of students so they better understand that all that they do works to transform them and helps with their engagement.

Self-serving Transformation

Through focus group discussions, it was made clear that there is a pattern that emerges, with students taking the first year to understand the university, the following one or two years to seek opportunities that are self-serving and then, finally, they might get engaged in activities that will benefit the community. There is a transformation of leadership from the student as an individual to the student getting involved in noble causes in a collaborative way. The influences outlined here are more about being a part of something big that makes one feel good. It is important to keep in mind that this is a generalization because there are students who start university and are fully engaged and, equally, there are students graduating who have made little progress in the engagement aspect of their degree.

Leadership Development and Academic Education

Academic education is a critical component of students' leadership development. It might not be direct and day-to-day, but it helps to establish their foundation of assessment, decision making and communication skills. I would argue that leadership development is more a combination of various internal and external factors that come together to form who we are and how we react to situations. We do not want to have institutions turning out one type of person to be a leader. A group needs diversity and variety in order to be effective. For example, an individual might be quiet but be able to contribute one aspect to the group dynamic, while another brings another set of experiences. Collectively, the group will therefore have a much more dynamic set of skills to apply to a problem or project. What is important to keep in mind in considering influences is that each person has had personal experiences that they bring to the group and this becomes the group's foundation.

Mission and Vision

For a student to have a focus on leadership development there is a need for the student to understand the mission and vision of a project. For a university, there is a need for the mission to be clear. SFU's mission statement is not accessible and from a student's perspective this is an example of the organization not having a clear mission, making it more difficult for students to have one. There is a need for the university to have an understood mission statement readily available, so that students can see what the university stands for and how the various parts of the academic studies and co-curricular aspects work together for their personal development.

Diversification

There are a few points to outline from a diversification standpoint. The university must understand that students have various priorities that shift depending on their academic education, work, and social life. These all factor into whether a student is influenced to get involved in an initiative or not. Students need to understand that, even if there are constraints upon them, there are still ways that they can make a valuable contribution to society. If school and work are involved, then it is a matter of a small contribution to the bigger project.

Related to the diversity issue is a need for the university administration to understand that there are students from various backgrounds who might not have the initiative or capacity to be involved because it is not in their social or cultural upbringing. Students need to seek out resources and it is the responsibility of the institution to provide those resources to foster engagement.

The Importance of This Study

Through the discussions and literature review, the objective was to determine what influences students to get involved or not and how the university might understand these influences. Understanding what has been derived from this study provides an environment that will allow university administrators to reflect on their own institutions and try to understand each other's perspectives in relation to student leadership development. The overall objective here is to provide a capacity for getting students involved and engaged so that all parties will benefit. The students will benefit by going forward as positive change agents in their respective communities, and by becoming stronger alumni and giving back to their institution. The university will benefit because it will be seen as an institution that has a foundation of leadership development giving back to the community and because it will have strong relationships with organizations that will in turn recognize the benefits that they provide.

List of References

Aldridge A. & Levine K. (2006). *Survey Methods: Pros and Cons.* Retrieved July 24, 2008, from http://www.nedarc.org/nedarc/media/pdf/surveyMethods_2006.pdf.

Donald G. (2008). *2008 From Learning to Work Report. Student Engagement Survey.* Unpublished Internal Report. Victoria, B.C.: Brain Storm Research.

Brungardt C.L. (1993). *The New Face of Leadership: Implications for Higher Education.* Kansas, Fort Hays State University. Retrieved July 2, 2001 from, Fort Hays State University Web site http://www.nwlink.com/~donclark/leader/lead_edu.html

Brungardt C.L. (1997). The Making of Leaders: A Review of the Research in Leadership Development and Education. *Journal of Leadership and Organizational Studies*, 3, 81-95.

Buchanan D. & Huczynski A. (2004). *Organizational Behavior: An Introductory Text.* Toronto: Prentice Hall.

Chrislip D.D. & Larson C.E. (1994). *Collaborative Leadership: How Citizens and Civic Leaders Can Make a Difference*, San Francisco: Jossey-Bass.

Chan L. (March 2000). *The Economic impact of Simon Fraser University on the Greater Vancouver Regional District.* Simon Fraser University.

Dunkle N. & Schuh J. (1998). *Advising Student Groups and Organizations.* San Francisco: Jossey-Bass.

Ghandi M.K. (1906) Quoted by Dr. Lawrence Edward Carter, October 2, 2003, at the Official Opening of the Gandhi-King-Ikeda Exhibit. Retrieved October 25, 2008 from http://www.gandhi.ca/carter.html

Gibbs G. (2007). *Analyzing Qualitative Data.* Los Angeles: Sage Publications.

Gill J. & Johnson P. (2002). *Research Methods for Managers.* London: Sage Publications.

Government of British Columbia, Ministry of Advanced Education and Labour Market Development (2008). *Post Secondary Central Data Warehouse Standard Reports – Gender.* British Columbia.

Grizzell B.C. (2008, Jan 9). Institutional Servant Leadership: A Catalyst for Urban Community Sustainability. *Academic Leadership Live*, Volume 6 – Issue 2.

Grint K. (2000). *Leadership: Classical, Contemporary and Critical Approaches.* Oxford: Oxford University Press.

Hamrick F.A., Evans N.J., & Schuh J.H. (2002). *Foundations of Student Affairs Practice.* San Francisco: Jossey-Bass.

Hess E.D. & Cameron K.S., (2006*). Leading with Values: Positivity, Virtue, and High Performance.* New York: Cambridge University Press.

Hoffman S.J., Rosenfield D., Gilbert J.H.V., & Oandasan I.F. (2008). Student Leadership in interprofessional education: benefits, challenges, and implications for educators and policy makers. *Blackwell Publishing Limited. Medical Education.* 42: pg 654-661.

Kaydos W. (1999). *Operational Performance Measurement: Increasing Total Productivity.* New York: St Lucie Press.

W.K. Kellogg Foundation (2000). *Leadership Reconsidered: Engaging Higher Education in Social Change.* Battle Creek, Michigan.

Komives S.R., Lucas N., & McMahon T.R (1998). *Exploring Leadership for College Students Who Want to Make a Difference.* San Francisco: Jossey-Bass.

Kotter J.P. (1996). *Leading Change.* Boston: Harvard Business School Press.

Kouzes J.M., & Posner B.Z. (2002). *The Leadership Challenge.* (3rd ed.). San Francisco: Jossey-Bass.

Kouzes J.M., & Posner B.Z. (2006). The *Five Practices of Exemplary Student Leadership.* San Francisco: Jossey-Bass.

Kruger M.L. (2007). School Leadership, Sex and gender: Welcome to Difference. *International Journal of Leadership in Education,* 11:2, 155-168.

Leonard E.F. (1998). Lead by Example and Precept: Introducing, Developing, and Recognizing Leadership Mastery at the Collegiate Level. *Journal of Leadership and Organizational Studies,* 4; 110-125.

Lin M.H. (2007). *Asian American Leadership Development: Examining the Impact of Collegiate Environments and Personal Goals,* University of California, Los Angeles, 2007. McDonald W. (2002). *Creating Campus Community.* San Francisco: Jossey-Bass.

McMillan J.H. & Schumacher S. (1989). *Research in Education: A Conceptual Introduction.* New York: Harper Collins Publishers.

McShane S.L. (2004). *Canadian Organizational Behavior.* Toronto: McGraw-Hill Ryerson, Toronto.

Morris D., & Tille. J. (2008, May). *Fall 2007 Undergraduate Student Survey: Report of Findings.* Burnaby: Simon Fraser University.

Mulinda J.M.V. (2008, May 12). The Leadership Paradox. *Academic Leadership*. Volume 6 – Issue 2.

Pierce J.L., & Newstrom J.W. (2006). *Leaders and the Leadership Process*. Toronto: McGraw-Hill Ryerson.

Portugal L.M. (2007, Feb 12). Diversity Leadership in Higher Education, *Academic Leadership*, Volume 4 – Issue 3.

Rowlands B.H. (2005). Grounded in Practice: Using Interpretive Research to Build Theory, *Electronic Journal of Business Research Methodology*, Vol. 3, Issue 1, page 81-92.

Sims R.R. & Quatro S.A., (2005). Leadership: Succeeding in the Private, Public, and Not-for-Profit Sectors. New York: M.E. Sharpe, Inc.

Simmons J.C., Grogan M., Preis S. J., Matthews K., Smith-Anderson S., Walls B.P., & Jackson A. (2007, Sept). Preparing First-Time Leaders for an Urban Public School District: An Action Research Study of a Collaborative District-University Partnership, *Journal of School Leadership*, Volume 17.

Sternberg R.J. (2005, Oct-Dec). A Model of Educational Leadership: Wisdom, Intelligence, and Creativity Synthesized, *International Journal of Leadership in Education*. Vol 8, No. 4, pg 355.

Stewart C. J., & Cash W.B jr. (1988). *Interviewing: Principles and Practices*, Iowa: Wm. C. Brown Publishers.

Stewart D., Shamdasani P., & Rook D. (2007) *Focus Groups – Theory and Practice*, Los Angeles: Sage Publications.

Taylor T., Martin B.N., Hutchinson S., & Jinks M. (2007, October 1) Examination of Leadership Practices of Principles Identified as Servant Leaders, *International Journal of Leadership in Education*. 10:4, 401-419.

Thiara A. 27 July, 2008, CLS Learning Log, Dissertation Entry.

Thiara A. 27 March, 2007, CLS Learning Log, Phase 3, Activity 3.

Thiara A. 20 May, 2007, CLS Learning Log, Phase 4, Week 1, Activity 2.

University of Exeter – (2007). Centre for Leadership Studies, Phase 2 – Week 4, Traditional Leadership Perspectives.

University of Exeter – (2007). Centre for Leadership Studies, Phase 2 – Week 5, Traditional Leadership Perspectives.

University of Toronto (2002, June 30). The Health Communication Unit, *Using Focus Groups, Version 2.0*. Retrieved July 17, 2008, from http://www.thcu.ca/infoandresources/publications/Focus_Groups_Master_Wkbk_Complete_v2_content_06.30.00_format_aug03.pdf

University of Windsor. (2006, December). *2006 National Survey of Student Engagement (NSSE)*. Windsor, Ontario.

Vecchio R.P. *Leadership: Understanding the Dynamics of Power and Influence in Organizations*. (2nd ed.) Indiana: University of Notre Dame Press.

Worthen B.R., & Sanders J.R. (1987). *Educational Evaluation: Alternative Approaches and Practical Guidelines*. New York: Longman.

Zaleznik A. (1990). *The Leadership Gap*, The Academy of Management Executive, 4(1), 12, pg 7-23.

Zimmerman-Oster K. & Burkhardt J.C. (1999). Leadership in the Making: A Comprehensive Examination of the Impact of Leadership Development Programs on Students, *Journal of Leadership and Organizational Studies*; 6; pg 50.

Appendices

Appendix A

List of Tables

Table 1 - Authors for the W.K Kellogg Paper

Primary Authors
• Alexander W. Austin • Helen S. Austin
Contributing Authors
• Kathleen E Allen • John C. Burkhardt • Christine M. Cress • Robert A. Flores • Philip Jones • Nance Lucas • Bonnie L. Pribush • William C. Reckmeyer • Bettye Parker Smith • Kathleen A. Zimmerman-Oster

Table 2 - Traditional Models of Leadership

The Trait Approach	Trait theories attempt to identify the inherent qualities of leaders and use them to inform recruitment development – The Great Man theory
The Skills Approach	This is somewhat related to the Trait theory but instead it focuses on the competencies of effective leaders
The Behavioural Approach	Behavioural theories concentrate on what leaders actually do rather than on their inherent qualities – showing leadership styles
The Situational (Contingency) Approach	This approach proposes that effective leadership depends on the situation in which it is being exercised and that the leader will need to adapt his/her style accordingly

(University of Exeter – Phase 2, Week 4)

Table 3 - Contemporary Models of Leadership

Charismatic Leadership	Focuses on the leader's role as a motivator of people and his/her ability to inspire followers
Transformational leadership	Contrasts transactional and transformational leadership. Transactional is useful for maintaining stability, transformational leadership is required during times of change, with the leader envisioning and implementing the transformation of organizational performance
The Leader as Follower	Sees the leader not as some exceptional individual 'out in front' but argues for the importance of 'leading quietly', 'servant leadership' and 'team leadership'
Distributed Leadership	Views leadership as a process that is diffused throughout an organization rather than lying solely with the formally designated 'leader'

(University of Exeter – Phase 2, Week 4)

Table 4 - Hersey and Blanshard Model

Directive Behaviour	<ul><li>One-way communication</li><li>Followers roles clearly defined</li><li>Close supervision of performance</li></ul>
Supportive Behaviour	<ul><li>Two-way communication</li><li>Listening, providing support and encouragement</li><li>Facilitate interaction</li><li>Involve followers in decision making</li></ul>

(University of Exeter – Phase 2, week 5)

Table 5 Academic and Practical Intelligence

Academic Intelligence	• Refers to memory and analytical abilities • Conventional notion of intelligence • Analyze, evaluate and judge information
Practical intelligence	• Ability to solve everyday problems by utilizing knowledge gained from experiences • Involves – managing self, managing others and managing tasks

(Sternberg, 2005, pg 355)

Table 6 Kotter's Eight-Stage Process of Creating Major Change

1) Establishing a sense of urgency
2) Creating the guiding coalition
3) Developing a vision and strategy
4) Communicating the change
5) Empowering broad-based action
6) Generating short-term wins
7) Consolidating gains and producing more change
8) Anchoring new approaches to the culture

(Kotter, 1996, pg 21)

Table 7 Applications to Integrate Student Leadership

1) Integration of students into larger curricular reform, research and policy initiative
2) Provision of support for the development of student-led IPE organizations (IPE – Inter-professional Education)
3) Establishing of partnerships with student organizations
4) Recognition for students when they make valuable contributions

(Hoffman, Rosenfield, Gilbert, and Oandasan, 2008, pg 659)

Table 8 – SFU Student Profile from 2007 SFU Undergraduate Survey

There are several noteworthy differences between the survey respondents and the population of all undergraduate students registered at SFU in the fall 2007 semester:

- On average, the survey respondents have a higher GPA
- 42% of respondents reported a GPA ≥ 3.00, whereas 26% of the student body actually has a GPA in that range.
- Females are over-represented (66%, versus 55% among all students)
- The respondents included more students with transfer credits (50%, versus 36% at SFU in general.)
- Due to these and other more minor differences, it is possible that the responses of survey participants are not completely representative of the population of all undergraduate students. Readers wishing to apply these results more broadly should bear that in mind.

Age	The average age of survey respondents was 22.4.
Basis of Admission	64% of respondents were admitted to SFU from high school, 29% transferred from a college or university, or had a BC Associate Degree, 2% were degree holders, 2% were mature, and 2% had another basis of admission.
Gender	About two thirds the survey respondents (66%) were female; 34% were male.
Year of Study	Based on transfer credits and SFU credits combined, 53% of respondents were in their first/second year and 47% were in the third/fourth/fifth year of their program. 28% of respondents stated that they were new to SFU this semester.

2008-05-29 Fall 2007 Undergraduate Student Survey: Report of Findings Page 5

Table 9 Gender demographics for focus group sessions

	Male	Female
% of male to female for all reporting institutions	47%	53%
Focus Group 1	64%	36%
Focus Group 2	71%	29%
Focus Group 3	66%	34%
Independent Responses	42%	58%

Table 10 – Breakdown of Focus Group Participants

Focus Group 1

Student	Year of Study	Faculty	Additional Faculty
1 - KS	4th	Arts	
2 - CS	4th	Business	
3 - SP	4th	Business	
4 - AB	4th	Business	
5 - ML	4th	Sciences	Business
6 - NC	4th	Business	
7 - SP	4th	Arts	Business
8 - CW	4th	Applied Science	Business
9 - JW	4th	Sciences	Business
10 - BS	3rd	Business	
11 - KB	4th	Business	

Focus Group 2

Student	Year of Study	Faculty	Additional Faculty
1 - JL	4th	Business	Arts
2 - FY	2nd	Business	
3 - HG	4th	Business	
4 - SR	4th	Business	
5 - SS	3rd	Business	Arts
6 - KL	4th	Business	
7 - KM	4th	Business	

Focus Group 3

Student	Year of Study	Faculty	Additional Faculty
1 - JM	4th	Arts	
2 - AP	2nd	Business	
3 - TW	4th	Business	
4 - JY	2nd	Business	
5 - SL	4th	Applied Science	
6 - MS	3rd	Business	
7 - MM	4th	Business	Arts
8 - GS	4th	Business	Arts
9 - RJ	4th	Business	

Table 11 - Fall 2007 Undergraduate Student Survey on students working

- 20.1% are committed to 11-15 hours a week
- 20.8% are involved in 16-20 hours a week
- 12.6% are doing 21-25 hours a week.
  (Simon Fraser University – Undergraduate Survey, Fall 2007, pg 53)

Are you working?	
Yes	2002 respondents – 61%
No	1278 respondents – 39%
Total	3280 respondents – 100%

Hours Worked per Week	Number of Students	% of students
Not working	11	0.6
1 – 5 hours	138	7.0
6 – 10 hours	353	17.8
11 – 15 hours	397	20.1
16 – 20 hours	411	20.8
21 – 25 hours	250	12.6
26 – 30 hours	117	5.9
31 – 35 hours	91	4.6
More than 40 hours	131	6.6
Total Respondents	**1980**	**100%**
Don't know	18	
Mission cases	4	

2008-05-29 Fall 2007 SFU Undergraduate Student Survey: Report of Findings Page 53

Appendix B

List of Figures

Figure 1 Five Key Areas of Relational Leadership

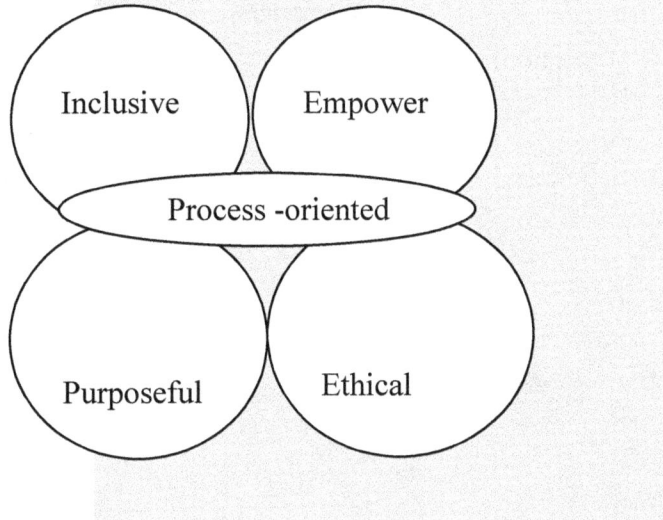

(Komives, Lucas and McMahon, 1998, pg 68-69)

Figure 2. Venn diagram to illustrate when students are focused on their studies near final exams

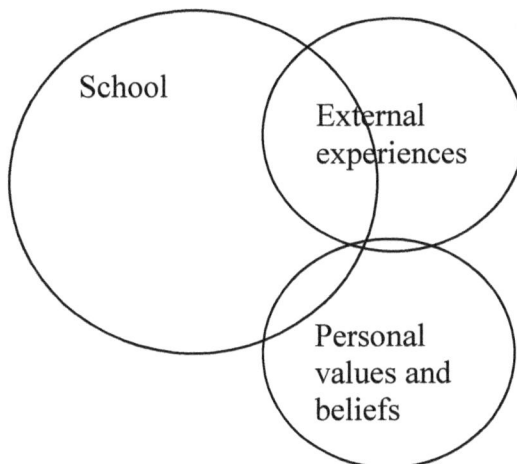

Figure 3. Venn diagram to illustrate Student Focus Between Semesters

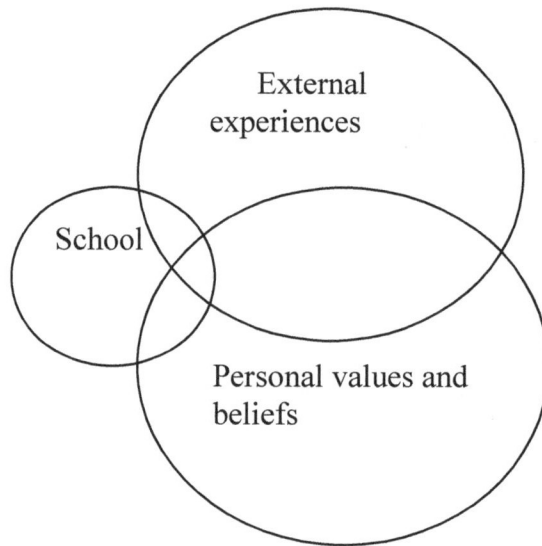

External experiences

School

Personal values and beliefs

Appendix C

Pre-Screening Form Sample

Student Leadership and Engagement – Pre-screening Form

You have been asked to take part in a study involving focus groups. The purpose of the focus group is to understand what influences students to get involved and to see how the university can leverage these influences to get further student engagement.

Please take a few minutes to outline information so that your suitability for the focus group can be assessed.

All information gathered will be in confidence and your information will not be shared with any third party agency. Please write your response or circle the most appropriate answer

Name: _____

My Year of study is: first year   second year

                             third year   fourth year

My Faculty is: Applied Science   Arts and Social Science

                        Business Administration   Education

                        Health Sciences   Science

My home status is: living on campus   living off campus

My age is: _____ years

My gender is: male   female

My ethnic background*: _____   (to help

determine which focus group)

* Ethnic background refers to your heritage and background. For example if your parents are from Europe and you were born in Canada, they you would indicate European/Canadian

Appendix D

Consent Form

My name is Sam (Ajit) Thiara, and I am the Student Affairs Officer for the Faculty of Business at Simon Fraser University. I am doing my Masters in Leadership Studies at the University of Exeter in England and am undertaking a study on leadership and what influences students to get involved.

You are being asked to participate in a research project involving focus groups. The focus of the study is to understand what influences university students to get involved, or not involved, and how can the university leverage the findings to create programs to get more students involved.

There will be three separate focus groups and you are being asked to be a participant of one of the groups. Each focus group will be no longer than two hours and will involve questions and discussions on leadership and community engagement.

All participant names will be coded to ensure confidentiality. Participation in the study will be strictly voluntary.

Participants have the option, at any time, to withdraw from the study and there will be no adverse effects on your grades, evaluations, course work or programs.

By consenting to participate in the focus group, you agree that any information you encounter will be kept confidential and not revealed to parties outside the focus group.

Research results or any complaints can be addressed to:

Dr. Hal Weinberg
Director, Office of Research Ethics
Office of Research Ethics
Simon Fraser University
8888 University Drive
Multi-Tenant Facility
Burnaby, B.C. V5A 1S6
hal_weinberg@sfu.ca

_____   _____
Participant Signature   Date

Appendix E

Questions for Focus Groups

Focus Group One and Two Guide Questions:

- How do you define leadership?
  - Do you consider yourself a leader or not
    - If yes, why
    - If no, why

- What influences you to either take on or not take on a leadership role?

- Describe a time when you took on a leadership role
  - What influenced you to take on the leadership role?

- Describe a time when you were part of a team member and not the leader
  - What influenced you to be a part of the team?

- Thinking in a general sense, what do you think might influence other people to take on a leadership role?

- Thinking in a general sense, what do you think might influence other people to not take on a leadership role?

- How can the university get more students involved?

- You have the opportunity to provide the university your advice on how to engage students in leadership roles, what is your message for the university?

Independent Response Supplementary Questions

1) What influences you to get involved (or not get involved) in community projects - community could be in school or outside school?

2) Where did the influence emerge from - is it external, cultural, over the years and developed...etc

3) What can a university do to further engage students - what do they need to do from a logistical perspective to leverage those influences that you just spoke about.

Focus Group Three Guide Questions:

Q – When you are involved in a project what are the things that you consider, or influence you, to take on a leadership role or participate as a team member and allow someone else to lead the project?

Q –How does the academic learning you do in class help to prepare you to take on a leadership role when you have to apply it to a practical community project.

Q –How does becoming more active in campus activities help you to develop as a leader?

Q – (Post-it note) Understanding that people around you make up who you are – do we then look for people like us or do we build off people we come across? In other words, who influences you?

Q – Look at mentorship and coaching – do you look for directional input (mentor) or guidance (coaching) when deciding on getting involved?

Q – (Post it notes) How can we demonstrate merit outside of the classroom and academic programs for the common good? For example start up a volunteer tutor group in finance for the purpose of helping other students achieve better grades.
Provide examples
What would influence you to take on such a leadership role?

Q –Faculty have an opportunity to build relationships with students and provide guidance and support. How do we engage faculty to take on a more active role outside of the classroom?

Q - With so many opportunities, why is it that students still don't get involved? What influences are present that causes someone to not get involved in a leadership role in campus activities.

Q – From the time you entered university to the present, and your engagement has increased, what made you change your focus from limited involvement to being more involved?
>   Did this make you a better leader?

Appendix F

Results from Brainstorm Survey – Reasons for students enrolling at SFU

Reasons for Enrolling

Why did you choose to enroll in college or university?

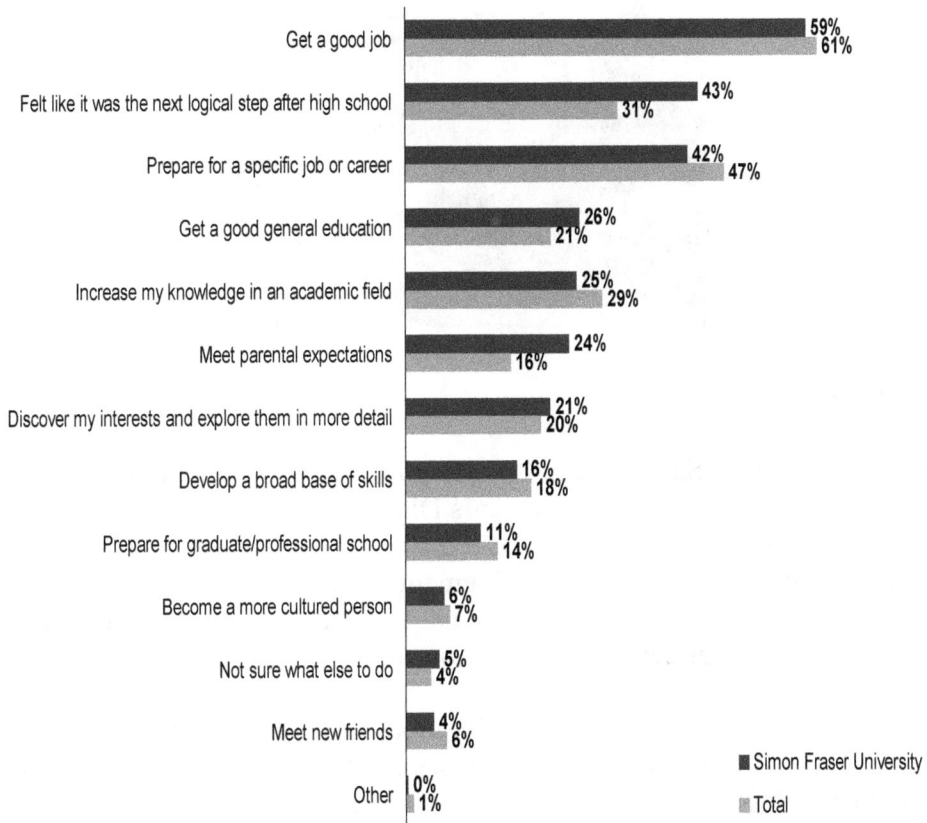

Reason	Simon Fraser University	Total
Get a good job	59%	61%
Felt like it was the next logical step after high school	43%	31%
Prepare for a specific job or career	42%	47%
Get a good general education	26%	21%
Increase my knowledge in an academic field	25%	29%
Meet parental expectations	24%	16%
Discover my interests and explore them in more detail	21%	20%
Develop a broad base of skills	16%	18%
Prepare for graduate/professional school	11%	14%
Become a more cultured person	6%	7%
Not sure what else to do	5%	4%
Meet new friends	4%	6%
Other	0%	1%

■ Simon Fraser University
▨ Total

DECODE
DECODING YOUTH, YOUNG ADULTS AND YOUNG FAMILIES

BRAINSTORM
STRATEGY | RESEARCH | TRAINING

UNIVERSUM
Building Brands to Capture Talent!

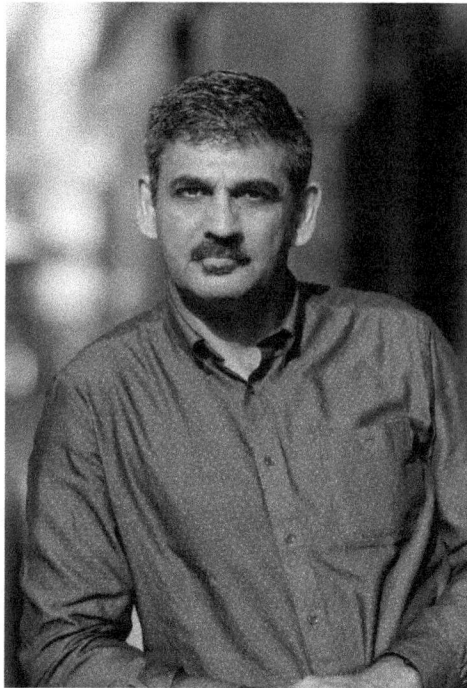

Sam's Story

Through his tireless work, Sam continues to be committed to the betterment of communities. In 2012 he received the Queen's Diamond Jubilee Medal, the Rick Hansen Difference Maker medallion and in 2006, the Governor General's Caring Canadian Award for leadership and community involvement. As a writer and blogger, his passion is to inspire and motivate others in their personal and professional development through his many adventures and reflections on life's journey.

Sam has mentored hundreds and engaged with thousands of students over the last many years and as a result, is Co-Founder and Chief Motivating Officer of GradusOne, an organization to help high school/post-secondary and recent graduates in their life and career. Since 2004, Sam found his calling at the Beedie School of Business at Simon Fraser University. His leadership role has always been to enhance the student, alumni, and young professional experience so they develop their personal brand. Sam has been creative and innovative in his approach to student/alumni engagement and has created countless opportunities for his audiences. As a lecture at the Beedie School of Business and Fraser International College, Sam has received exemplary ratings. He possess a keen interest in the international student area and helping the students succeed both academically, professionally and personally. Sam created a conversation skills workshop series to help students on their soft skills as this is vitally important to help international students transition.

Added to this, Sam is an accomplished speaker and storyteller. As a result, he helped create and speaks for SoapBox Speakers. Either as a mentor/coach to a single student or speaking to hundreds as a keynote speaker, he shares his experiences through storytelling and has helped thousands in the pursuit of their dreams. In 2011, Sam delivered a TEDxSFU speech about 'Discovering the Extraordinary in the Ordinary'. This then led to a published book on personal storytelling and helping the reader build their story-voice – https://www.lulu.com/shop/search.ep?keyWords=sam+thiara&type=

Prior to SFU, Sam was part of the Vancouver 2010 Olympic Bid Committee and ICBC road safety where it was about about community building. With 40 + volunteer organizations that Sam has been involved with from the board, advisory to volunteer level, he has dedicated countless hours to his communities. Presently, he is working with a refugee community in Kenya to help them vision a sustainable plan and a school program for the children.

Sam completed his Masters in Leadership Studies at the University of Exeter in England, has a double major in Business Administration and Political Science from SFU, completed a certificate in Life Coaching from Cambridge University, a community leadership program through Leadership Vancouver, a Human Resources certificate from BCIT, and adult education certification with Vancouver Community College.

Sam consistently strives to discover the extraordinary in the ordinary and his journey is documented at http://sam-thiara.com His favourite saying and what he lives by: *"Everyone's life is an autobiography...make yours worth reading!"*

Please feel free to connect with Sam to talk about your personal journey or your educational institution.

Email – story.share.community@gmail.com

Linked In - https://ca.linkedin.com/in/sthiara

Twitter - @Sam_Thiara

Instagram - SamThiara

www.ingramcontent.com/pod-product-compliance
Lightning Source LLC
Chambersburg PA
CBHW081333090426

42737CB00017B/3118